I0172805

The Masculine Creator

How a Man Becomes a Maker of World Makers

By: Clarity

Copyright © 2021 Clarity

All rights reserved.

ISBN: 978-1-941192-04-7

Table of Contents

Introduction

It is good to be a man, a truth first proclaimed by the Creator on the sixth day and a truth that—despite current conjecture—remains unaltered to the present day. First, we'll consider how a man becomes a unique embodiment of the Masculine Creator by defining himself as one who is unlike anyone else. Then, we'll explore the potential for a man selecting a spouse so that he might become one, leading two toward becoming unlike anyone. Lastly, we'll outline a fully mature embodiment of the Masculine Creator who mentally inspires, emotionally enthralls, and physically empowers everyone toward becoming a unique one so that all humanity might return to being a race of unique world makers who are each making their own unique world for God's world of unique worlds.

Part 1
A Self-Defining Authority

Since each male materially bears the World Maker's likeness, each man intuitively works toward establishing himself as the one and only maker of his own unique world. However, the moment a man attempts to break away from convention to establish his own sovereign domain, he'll be assaulted from all sides. Therefore, a man's first step in defining his masculinity is to forcefully repulse everyone and everything so he might rule, fill, and subdue his own unique world. A self-defining man leaves behind every pre-existing world, to go forth and create his own world, so that—one day—he might return with the means to enrich and expand all worlds.

Section 1
The Dedicated Man

A dedicated man begins his world-making endeavor by rejecting every world as a possible home, thereby obligating him to strike out and orchestrate his own. A boy's first step on the path to manhood is learning how to execute a self-defined decision. Then, he transitions into adolescence by facing the ominous and inescapable burden of his masculine life debt. Finally, a male becomes a man by executing his self-defined decision to make his own unique world that is specifically designed to serve the survival, comfort, and orchestration of every unique one within God's race of unique world makers.

Chapter 1
A Self-Defined Decision

A self-defined decision requires a man to ask and answer three sequential questions without assistance. The first question is, "Does it need to be done?" The second is, "Who will see it done?" And the third and final question is, "How far will I go to get it done?"

As a boy, a male expects others to tell him what needs to be done, who should get it done, and how far to go to ensure it is done. An undeveloped male cannot establish, energize, or execute his own decisions, thereby making him dependent upon the authority of others. Therefore, a boy establishes his masculinity as he rejects the authority of others in preparation for establishing himself as his own authority.

A young man rightfully takes pride in being the only authority over his soul, his body, and his world. While maturing into adolescence, he'll delight in deciding for himself how to do things and how far to go in seeing them through to completion. However, he'll not be recognized as a man—by himself or others—until he also takes the vital first step in deciding what needs to be done. The one who decides what needs to be done, takes full responsibility to get it done, and commits to getting it done or dying in his attempt is a man.

The "it" within a man's self-defined decision always refers to the same thing. Since a man embodies the World Maker, the only thing any man is interested in creating is his own unique world. Therefore, when a man asks himself, "Does it need to be done?" he is merely asking, "Does my world need to be created?" The answer, should a man seek external guidance, will be utter silence. Since a man's world does not yet exist, no one else will be able to vouch for the validity of his intentions. Even if a man attempts to beseech the highest authority for a decision regarding whether or not to make his world, he'll likewise find God frustratingly silent. The privilege—and burden—of bearing the World Maker's likeness demands that a man looks to no one other than himself when deciding whether or not to make his own unique world.

God decided to create His world without the opinions, encouragements, or validations of others. Instead, God established, energized, and executed His own self-defined decision based exclusively upon His own authority. Any man who wishes to uniquely embody the Masculine Creator must do likewise.

A man has only two options when considering whether or not to orchestrate his own unique world. He can either remain silent—to smolder in self-pity at his cowardice—or give voice to the one and only answer. Still, every man initially hesitates when considering the merits of striking out to orchestrate his own never-before-seen world. After all, every man doubts his ability to make the right decision.

Every man raised by fallen men has been bludgeoned from infancy with the importance of making the right decisions while avoiding the wrong decisions. At the same time, no fallen man has ever been able to precisely articulate exactly what separates a right decision from a wrong decision. Fortunately, the Masculine Creator does not require a man to make the right decisions, for only One can achieve such a standard. Instead, God expects each man to make his own decisions which, consequently, is exactly how the Right One makes His decisions.

Masculinity is not about being good and avoiding evil. Masculinity is about being unique. The tree bearing the forbidden fruit bore its name for a reason. Any effort to be good or avoid evil forces a man to conform to pre-existing forms of good or evil, thereby inhibiting him from becoming unique.

Being unique is the third option for a man to pursue. The first option is to be good. The second option is to not be evil. However, the third option is what God had originally intended each man to pursue before our rebellion. Only after a man turns away from pursuing good and avoiding evil may he approach the One who can make him into a unique one. Being one who is unlike anyone and creating a world that is unlike any other requires a man to completely separate his soul from anything or anyone other than the Unique One.

While lingering upon the precipice of a self-defined decision, a man will find himself staring into the void from which his world might one day rise. From such a vantage, a man must count the cost. Eventually, he'll rightly conclude that striking out on his own to create his own never-before-seen world will cost him everything. However, he'll also realize that not pursuing the manifestation of his own sovereign domain will leave him in his present state of having nothing, being nowhere, and existing as no one for all eternity. Under the weight of such revelations, a male becomes a man as he steps off into the void to create his own unique world from amidst God's world.

"Does it need to be done?" A man knows the answer. However, "Who will see it done?" While young, males look to others to ensure their survival, comfort, and orchestration. After maturing into adolescence, a male will naturally begin striving to ensure his own survival, comfort, and orchestration. However, all adolescent males hesitate under the ever-increasing burden of masculinity. Once a male realizes that he exists not only to make his own unique world but to make his own unique world that will make unique world makers, he'll know the one and only answer to the second question in his self-defined decision.

When God first created His world, He began with a material void. Similarly, each man must consciously leave all pre-existing worlds to go forth and select a void from which he might summon forth his own unique world. Unfortunately, no remnant of the original material void remains. Still, there is hope. Our Creator intentionally implants a void in each man sufficient to summon forth an entire domain of personal distinction. However, the void a man harbors is not material but spiritual.

Every soul is crafted by God as a spiritual void of infinite emptiness. Therefore, each soul is a boundless expanse of world-making potential. However, a man cannot use the spiritual void within him to make his material world. Instead, a man's soul carries the spiritual void from which God will make a unique world maker. Then, as a unique world maker, a man may go forth to make his own material world. After all, a unique world maker must exist before a unique world may manifest.

Similar to how God's touch upon the original material void created a unique world, so God's touch upon a man's spiritual void will create a unique world maker. Once God is touching, shaping, and breathing a unique world maker into existence—from within a man's soul—then a man will be able to go forth to do likewise by touching, shaping, and breathing upon his personal portion of God's material world to bring forth his own unique world.

As a masculine creator, a man looks only to himself when creating his own unique world. However, a man's first issue is to become a unique world maker, which requires him to look to God alone for the touch that will animate and illuminate his vacuous soul. First, the World Maker must conceive a spiritual world maker. Then, as a spiritual world maker, a man may go forth to create his own material world from amidst the world that God designed to become humanity's world of unique worlds.

Presently, the touch of Light, Love, and Life is reserved exclusively for making unique world makers, not making unique worlds. God does not wish to determine what a man should build, who should build it, and how far he should go to ensure its completion. God desires to spiritually make unique world makers who—as unique beings of world-making authority—will determine for themselves what to do, who should do it, and how far to go. Any man looking to others to make any aspect of his self-defined decision has yet to fully embrace his masculinity.

A man knows that there is only one who will see to the orchestration of his unique world. There is no one else. Not even God will build a man's world for him. Although a man must spiritually surrender his soul to God that is only because he must first be made into a spiritual world maker before attempting to make his material world. Following God's spiritual insemination, a man stands alone to exert his own material touch that will define, decide, and direct the orchestration of his sovereign domain.

The last question in a man's self-defined decision, just like the first two, leads to only one inevitable answer. A man knows that the completion of his world will cost him everything. The desire to form a visionary plan, produce meaningful labor, and complete a principal purpose through one grand, world-making effort is the end of every man. Consequently, no more visionary, meaningful, and purposeful task exists than creating one's own unique world. Therefore, the answer for how far a man should go in creating his world is always the same: to the death.

Men naturally dream about laying their life down to protect the woman they love. However, a woman is the embodiment of feminine creation. As a result, men naturally default to depicting a woman as the object of their sacrificial offering because depicting the entire universal whole of creation's anatomical splendor is a bit overwhelming. Similar to how a male body materially represents the Masculine Creator, so a female body materially represents Mother Nature. Although a man might conceptualize a woman as the object of his protective love, she is merely the personification—and potentially, his foremost human partner—in the orchestration of what he truly loves, his own unique world specifically designed to make unique world makers.

The man who executes his own self-defined decision sets himself on a path that will lead to the completion of his world. As he begins moving forward, a man will find himself buffeted, assaulted, and abused by all those who doubt him as a unique one capable of creating his own unique world. Unsurprisingly, no one else will be able to see the world a man envisions. Only the man himself, who has made the decision by himself, will be able to see, feel, and experience the world he intends to bring forth.

As a man moves toward the orchestration of his unique world, he'll inevitably find himself on his back with a dazed mind, a broken heart, and a bruised body. Amidst such moments—which are likely to be nearly every moment—a masculine creator will once again make his self-defined decision. While teetering on the verge of oblivion, a man will ask himself, yet again, "Does it need to be done?" causing his eyes to open. Then, the second question will follow more quickly and more forcefully, "Who will see it done?" After gritting his teeth against the pain, a man will rise to his feet and pause only long enough to ask the final question in his self-defined decision, "How far will I go to get it done?" Then, as a man steps forward, he'll sense the natural world around him awakening, seemingly eager to assist him in fulfilling his one and only desire as a masculine creator.

Chapter 2
The Masculine Life Debt

The first man chose a life of independence from God. As a result, all men must now toil, suffer, and fail to create their world within God's world without God's touch. After all, attempting to make a unique world without first being made into a unique world maker is a doomed effort. Additionally, God has cursed creation—because of the first man—obligating her to obstruct every man. Therefore, the purpose of each man's masculine life debt is for him to toil, suffer, and fail all his days so that he might know—and never forget—the cost of independence from God.

When considering humanity's fall, the cost of choosing spiritual independence from God does not initially appear dire. In fact, we even gained the ability to judge the difference between good and evil. Through our illicitly gained knowledge, each man now has the opportunity to present himself as the Good One by judging everything and everyone else as evil. Unfortunately, by systematically proclaiming every aspect of God's world as evil, to contrastively portray himself as Good, each man engenders even more disdain from creation. As a result, the toil, suffering, and failure each man is bound to experience have become, not only an unavoidable certainty but an inescapable reality.

Mother Nature detests anyone with the temerity to judge any aspect of her anatomical splendor as evil due to God having already proclaimed every atom of her universal whole as equally, unalterably, and eternally good. Creation despises any man lost in the delusion of being the One who is Good as he touches, shapes, and breathes upon her atoms with the intent to destroy her, remake her, and enthrone himself as the new and improved Good One. Therefore, our material mother venomously obstructs each man amidst her material realm, as well as within each man's own inner realm of mind, heart, and body. After all, everything made of atoms is creation. Consequently, every fallen man eventually discovers that he—as a spiritual soul—is imprisoned inside a hostile anatomical domain enslaving him to endless toil, ever-increasing suffering, and world-making failure.

The consequence of humanity pursuing independence from God was the removal of every soul from God's touch. Tragically, without the Creator inseminating each soul to bring forth a sovereign being of unique world-making authority, we each remain a lifeless void of infinite spiritual emptiness. Presently, we do not recognize the gravity of such a loss because our virgin void has never birthed a unique one, prohibiting us from recognizing the loss of something that we never had in the first place. Still, we do get a sense that something is off due to our minds being unable to perceive like unique ones, our hearts being unable to feel like a unique ones, and our bodies being unsure how to act as unique ones. Without a spiritual being of unique world-making authority awakened by God's touch from within each soul, no one can uniquely think, feel, and act their way toward making their own unique world.

Humanity's spiritual independence from God has condemned every soul to remain a non-existent void of infinite spiritual emptiness. The reason children, women, and creation routinely ignore a man's leadership is due to them not being able to see, feel, or experience a unique one of masculine authority inside his masculine body. Although all do recognize each male as bearing the material likeness of the Masculine One, no one innately perceives any man as a unique spiritual authority capable of leading, protecting, and inspiring them toward making their own unique world within God's world of unique worlds.

A fallen man blames children, women, and creation for failing to recognize him as a unique, world-making authority. Then, he foolishly wastes his entire life trying to prove that the reason no one recognizes him as an authority is because he actually is the Authority. Sadly, the more a man pressures everyone toward acknowledging him as the One, the more he convinces everyone that he is no one.

Despite being an untouched soul of infinite spiritual emptiness, each man naively believes that he'll figure out how to think, feel, and act uniquely. Unfortunately, there is only one who is Unique. Although fallen men innately recognize this truth, their strategy to rectify their lack of uniqueness is to replicate the Unique One. However, anyone who is attempting to replicate another is, by definition, not a unique one.

A woman who embodies feminine creation enjoys the benefit of being able to model the beautiful, nurturing, and wrathful forms of Mother Nature. However, a man has no such luxury. The Masculine Creator is spiritual, not material. The first man's choice—to pursue full spiritual independence from God—has prohibited every subsequent male from personally experiencing the Masculine One.

No man can summon forth a unique spiritual being from within his soul. Every untouched soul will remain just like everyone else, a spiritual void that is nothing, nowhere, and no one. Additionally, any spiritual void touching itself can only spawn an ever-increasing spiritual void. Worse yet, a vacuous soul touching their own mind, heart, and body will obligate their inner realm to express their lightless, loveless, and lifeless nature. Creation's atoms always crumble toward death and back into the dust while expressing a lifeless, untouched, and vacuous soul.

Each man born spiritually independent from God engenders a masculine debt to toil, suffer, and fail all his life. Consequently, a life that produces nothing is a suitable material expression of an untouched spiritual soul who is nothing. Mother Nature's material expressions are always obedient approximations of what is contained within every soul.

19

No man escapes his masculine life debt. Each man must toil, suffer, and fail all his days so he might know he is not the Unique One. Only as a man consensually bears his masculine life debt will he consider returning to the One capable of making him, also, unlike anyone.

Any man who attempts to stop paying his masculine life debt will find Mother Nature and her human counterparts working overtime toward ensuring what spiritually resides within his soul attains robust material expression. Feminine creation—and the women who embody her likeness—harbor an acute vindictiveness against any man who does not work all his life to see, feel, and experience the material fullness of his spiritual emptiness. Our material mother expects each man to strive and to fail in creating his own unique world within her as God's world of unique worlds. When the first man rebelled from God, creation was dragged kicking and screaming with humanity into our rebellion. Today, she remains kicking and screaming at any man who continues to make the same choice as the first man.

Out of righteous spite, creation intentionally entices each man toward her limitless world-making potential, only to utterly deny him world-making success. Each time a man's soul touches a single atom of Mother Nature, he'll find his efforts culminating in darkness, decay, and death. Additionally, women also follow our mother's example by pulling men close, only to utterly deny them access to and control over their limitless world-making potential.

The man who lives spiritually independent from God is both a lifelong tragedy and an eternal tragedy. In contrast, the man who returns his soul to God will remain a lifelong tragedy while enjoying a far different experience in the age of creators yet to come. Amidst the present age, our cursed, corrupted, and condemned orchestrational mother must ensure the toil, suffering, and failure of every man. Even the man who spiritually returns his soul to God will not escape this fate.

God's curse upon creation requires her to maintain a ceaseless wrath against all men. Only after creation has been remade, and the original world-making partnership is reformed between the Creator, creation, and every human creator may all return to making a world of unique worlds.

Still, the greatest tragedy for a man is to live his entire life without ever understanding why he's failed to make his unique world. Fallen men blame everything and everyone other than themselves. Enlightened men blame their own minds, hearts, and bodies. However, a resurrected man blames only his lightless, loveless, and lifeless soul. The man who willfully shoulders his masculine life debt and properly identifies the whole of humanity's fall as stemming from his soul alone will take it upon himself to pay his masculine life debt in a way that leads all through the present age of death and dust and on into the age of creators yet to come.

Originally, a man was designed to live materially independent from creation while remaining spiritually dependent upon the Creator. However, the first man chose spiritual independence from God, unaware that doing so would make him materially dependent upon creation. Full independence, both material and spiritual, is not an option for any human being. As created ones, we must be dependent upon someone or something. Once we turned away from the spiritual Creator, the only thing left for our souls to cling to was material creation.

As free-willed creatures who bear both a spiritual and a material nature, each must decide where they'll be dependent and where they'll be independent. The first man chose independence from our spiritual Father, which instantly made him dependent upon our material mother. Sadly, since he was the first man from whom all men would follow, his decision became every man's decision. Fortunately, God came as a man to become the Man, so He might return the decision of independence to every man. Now, each man must decide to remain spiritually independent from God and materially dependent upon creation or return to spiritual dependence upon God to achieve material independence from creation.

Our material mother was never designed to sustain spiritual beings. She was designed to express spiritual beings. Mankind's spiritual emancipation from God effectively spilled billions of untouched spiritual voids across the glorious anatomical expanse of our orchestrational mother. Now, each soul drains the light, love, and life from material creation that we were supposed to be receiving from the One who is spiritual Light, Love, and Life. As our mother wilts beneath the vampiric effect of our souls, we collectively cry out in distress at the insufficiency of her finite material nature.

A man's dependence upon material substances, material objects, material relationships, material aspirations, material money, and anything else made of atoms is an incomprehensible humiliation. Fallen men drain their wives, children, country, employer, parents, house, dreams, and even their own minds, hearts, and bodies of anatomical effervescence in a doomed attempt to animate their own lightless, loveless, and lifeless souls. However, a soul is not created to feed upon creation. Each soul is created to feed upon the Creator, so each might become a unique one who can then turn to feed creation with their uniqueness. After all, a void of infinite emptiness may only receive satiation from Infinite Fullness.

A man attains material independence from creation by returning to spiritual dependence upon the Creator. At the same time, a man must willfully pay his masculine life debt to toil, suffer, and fail as a world maker so he might know his ceaseless need for the World Maker. Then, as a man spiritually awakens as a living authority of light, love, and life, he may mentally inspire, emotionally enthrall, and physically empower every other soul toward also returning to God so each might become a unique one amidst God's race of unique world makers and return to making the world that only they can make, for God's world of unique worlds.

Chapter 3
A Man's Value

The man touched by God willfully pays his masculine life debt by creating a world that he knows will not last to ensure the survival, comfort, and orchestration of all. Although a man must toil, suffer, and ultimately fail in creating a lasting world within God's world, that does not stop him from directing his doomed orchestrational effort toward preserving the one thing that will retain its value from this age and into the age of creators yet to come. Consequently, the only thing God will carry into the coming age of creators—as it exists in the present age—are the spiritual world makers He makes from within each submissive soul.

When the World Maker touches our soul's void of infinite emptiness, a world maker is conceived with the independence, authority, and uniqueness needed to make their own unique world. Then, as our spiritual dependence upon God steadily increases, we're progressively freed from our material dependence upon creation. A man's growing independence from creation is what allows him to authoritatively lead his personal portion of Mother Nature away from her present anatomical forms and toward the anatomical forms required for his unique world.

God makes spiritual world makers. Then, as one spiritually made by the World Maker, a man may go forth to materially make a world designed to lead humanity toward being a race of unique world makers. In the same way that the Masculine Creator works to ensure humanity's spiritual survival, comfort, and orchestration so each masculine creator works to ensure humanity's material survival, comfort, and orchestration. God expects each man to ensure each soul touched by Him attains full maturity as a spiritual, inner, and material world maker. Our Creator desires this partnership with every man, and every man desires this partnership with his Creator. Unfortunately, the first man turned away from his partnership with God. As a result, each man now only works to ensure his own survival, comfort, and orchestration, thereby completely missing the purpose of his masculinity.

God did not intervene in the first man's choice because He was, and still is, intrinsically invested in the self-determination of our species. Creating independent, authoritative, and unique world makers requires keeping everyone free from external control. The Infinite One knew that any of His direct interventions in the finite material realm would infringe upon the ecosystem of self-determination that He created to cultivate the free-willed, eternal world-making partners He desires.

When God did take a more hands-on approach to the human problem, He did not do so as God but as a man. The Infinite One entered the material realm as a finite man to keep from disturbing Mother Nature as His eco-system for self-determining souls while also reclaiming the position abandoned by the first man. Even after our fall, our Creator remained undeterred in His desires for humanity to continue leading His world of unique worlds as His race of unique world makers. Each man who returns his soul to the Authority will awaken as an authority capable of leading our species back into our original partnership with our spiritual Father and our material mother.

Every human world maker requires three things if they are to temporarily create their own unique world within God's world: survival, comfort, and orchestration. These three things are provided spiritually by the Masculine Creator and materially by each masculine creator. At the same time, each man is finite. Therefore, no man may ensure the material survival, comfort, and orchestration of every world, any world, or even his own world. Instead, each masculine one must design a world that will bring forth one unique form of survival, comfort, or orchestration for all worlds. Any man who pays his masculine life debt by providing humanity with something everyone needs will spend the remainder of his days cultivating the unique ones eternally treasured by the Unique One.

A man's first option—to pay his masculine life debt—is to design a world that will serve in the survival of every world maker and their world amidst God's world. Amidst the present fallen age, where everyone is hostile and, occasionally, homicidal, everyone values a man capable of uniquely ensuring their survival. Traditionally, men who desire to ensure the survival of all select fields of employment such as farming, law enforcement, or the military. Such occupations allow a man to work toward everyone's continuing existence amidst creation's material realm.

The fields of employment focused on survival are notoriously underpaid. However, this is by design. The men who ensure humanity's survival must, themselves, remain on the razor's edge of life and death. A farmer should never stray too far from the soil from which all things grow and to which all things return. A police officer should never lose touch with the pulse of the streets, lest that day be his last. And a soldier should never venture too far from the trenches that protect him and allow him to hold the line. Society has always paid its masculine masters of survival only enough to allow them to survive but not enough to allow them to grow sloppy, civilized, or careless. Consequently, when men do move up the pay scales within the employment fields of survival, they have a strong tendency to stop working toward the survival of all as they start working toward the survival of only one.

A man who pays his masculine life debt by ensuring everyone survives will receive far more than a petty salary. A masculine master of survival protects, preserves, and procures what matters most for world-making. After all, a spiritual being devoid of a material body cannot create their own unique world. Therefore, the man who works to put food on the table, protects against the elements, or wards off aggressors will experience a life of supreme intimacy with those who look to him for their survival. Although a masculine master of survival will generally receive less pay for the invaluable service he provides, he'll end up being the most honored and beloved of men.

A man may produce whatever form of value he wishes to pay his life debt provided others find what he produces valuable for their survival, comfort, and orchestration. When a man fails to create a form of value that others recognize as valuable, he'll be offered and, if resistant, eventually forced into taking a job. However, every man innately resents employment, since accepting such a position means he'll be working on the world of another rather than on his own world. The norm for employed men is to ceaselessly complain, belittle, and deride their employer as the one who is obstructing them from creating their own unique world. However, such subversive efforts only serve to hide a man's self-inflicted state of enslavement to another man's world.

Human society and creation collectively assume that the only reason a man is not creating anything valuable is that he doesn't know how. Therefore, they will forcibly move any unproductive man toward employment within a productive man's world in the hope that he might learn to do likewise. The man who fails to create a unique world producing anything valuable and who also refuses employment beneath one who is will be discarded by society, creation, and the Creator. The Masculine Creator is always working toward the survival, comfort, and orchestration of every soul in the spiritual realm. He expects each man bearing His likeness to do likewise in the material realm.

Alongside the perils inherent to surviving our fallen age are the challenges of ensuring everyone's comfort. The men who choose to live as humanity's masculine masters of comfort will pay their life debt by constructing ecosystems of contentment around each human being so that all might create the profound thoughts, potent emotions, and powerful actions they need to make their unique world. Surviving comfortably is absolutely indispensable for a world maker. A comfortable environment is what allows a creator to weather the mental, emotional, and physical strains inherent to designing, building, and maintaining a never-before-seen world. Consequently, the man who pays his life debt by providing a unique form of comfort to all will be sought by all.

Human beings who live in a state of discomfort often resent those living a more comfortable life. However, their resentment toward those who are comfortable is based upon their own desire for more comfort. Life's comforts are neither good nor evil. However, they are essential for any human mind, heart, and body engaged in a world-making effort. A masculine master of comfort knows that surrounding each soul with the comforts customized to their world-making effort is vital for their world and every world their world will eventually serve.

Traditionally, a man who wishes to pay his life debt by ensuring everyone's comfort selects a field of employment like invention, manufacturing, or transportation. Spending one's life conceptualizing, building, or distributing life's comforts leads all toward a world of unique worlds. Generally, a masculine master of comfort will receive higher pay than a masculine master of survival. We want those who ensure our comfort to be ready at a moment's notice to intervene the moment we begin experiencing discomfort. Once our world needs a new idea, an appliance repaired, or immediate delivery of a vital supply, we want our masculine masters of comfort to respond without delay. Keeping a man in a constant state of readiness to rectify humanity's discomforts requires compensating him enough so that he might keep his own mind, heart, and body free of discomfort.

The hostile material realm of creation and the contentious interactions of human society require men who will ceaselessly work toward ensuring everyone's comfort. Without men customizing comfortable environments, no one will be able to create their own unique world that serves every other world maker and their world amidst God's world. As a result, the man who serves humanity as a masculine master of comfort will end up being the most respected and trusted of men.

No man can better himself, his life, or even his world by ensuring the survival, comfort, or orchestration of others. Everything a man touches will eventually return to dust, expressing how he began his life as one who is spiritually nothing, nowhere, and no one. Therefore, a man does not pay his life debt to attain gain for himself or others. Instead, a man pays his life debt so the Masculine Creator might gain the submissive souls He desires. A man ensures humanity's material survival, comfort, and orchestration so each might have the opportunity to decide for themselves to either return to spiritual dependence upon God or remain eternally independent from Him.

Humanity's masculine masters of survival and comfort work together to ensure everyone is surviving comfortably. Then, the final group of men may pay their life debt in a way that enables everyone to temporarily orchestrate their world within God's world. Amidst survival, comfort, and orchestration, the highest pay scales are usually reserved for humanity's masters of orchestration. The reason we pay the final category of men so handsomely is that we want them to never have to worry about their survival or comfort as they stick their heads in the clouds to oversee the vast complex systems allowing everyone to create their world within God's world of unique worlds.

God's world is complex. Successfully planning, building, and maintaining the systems that allow billions of unique world makers to co-exist requires undistracted masters of orchestration wrestling with those complexities. The men who intend to ensure humanity's orchestrational efforts traditionally select fields of employment like politics, logistics, or theoretics. Although many men see the higher pay of such jobs as desirable, few are willing to pay the price of loneliness that often accompanies such labors. A society intuitively avoids distracting those who uphold the complex systems that enable everyone's utilities, social structures, and technologies. Additionally, orchestrational masters also have a strong tendency to grow aloof from society as they get lost in the intoxicating complexities of their work.

God's world is not only complex but utterly hostile to every human being. While humanity's masters of survival and comfort work to keep everyone alive and at ease, it falls to the masculine masters of orchestration to figure out how to lead a race of replicated world takers back toward being a race of unique world makers. Orchestrational masters strategize, monetize, and allegorize clever means that will allow each rebellious soul to temporarily make their own world within God's world. Although a masculine master of orchestration is more likely to experience a financially blessed life, he is also more likely to experience deep loneliness despite being the most revered and renowned of men.

Together, humanity's masculine masters of survival, comfort, and orchestration each pay their life debt in a way that upholds God's original vision for a race of unique world makers who, together, are bringing forth a world of unique worlds. Each masculine creator lives and dies to protect, procure, and preserve everyone as a unique one. No man may make anyone else's world. However, each man may make his world to provide a unique form of survival, comfort, or orchestration to every world and every world maker so that the World Maker might acquire what He desires most.

Section 2
The Defiant Man

The man who pays his life debt by sacrificially providing
humanity with one unique form of survival, comfort, or orchestration
must also heft the even greater burdens of masculine truth, leadership,
and duty. Each man grows into his own likeness of the Masculine One as
he progressively faces and then embraces the one truth he's always
known—and always feared. Then, a man may defiantly lead our species
of world takers through the death and dust of the present age toward
becoming a growing race of unique world makers. Consequently, each
man who knows the doomed nature of our present will partner with God
to ensure everyone has their chance to return to the One who will make
them, protect them, and preserve them for the age of creators yet to
come.

Chapter 4
The Unalterable Truth

Every man is born knowing he is a worthless failure. Although men do not know why they perceive, feel, and experience themselves in such a way, it is this innate knowledge that drives every man to waste his entire life attempting to disprove the only truth he's ever known. Still, eventually, every man is forced—by life's hardships or death's embrace—to face the unalterable truth.

Although a man cannot alter the heritage of failure endowed upon him by the first man, the possibility of returning to Success remains open. Unfortunately, any man who returns to the Successful One must first face the truth that he is not the Successful One. The reason every man is born knowing he is a worthless failure is that, like the first man, every man knows that he's failed to make himself like God.

Each man is presently running from the unalterable truth. Any time he woos a woman, hoists a trophy, or attains anything of merit, a man will find himself drowning amidst the same unaltered revelation. As every man eventually discovers, attaining material success does not alter his spiritual state of failure.

God is masculine success because He alone is unlike anyone. Men fail as masculine beings because we're all trying to replicate the Unique One. Instead, when a man spiritually bows before God, he does so by first facing and then embracing the unalterable truth that He has failed to make himself Unique.

Without God's touch, every soul remains a spiritual void of infinite emptiness who is nothing, nowhere, and no one. A soul is designed by God to only respond to His touch. However, when God's insemination conceives a unique spiritual being from within our submissive soul, He does not make a replica of Himself. Rather, the Unique One's touch upon our soul makes one who is also unlike anyone.

The first man chose to pursue independence from God amidst his naive hope that he might find the material means to make himself into a replica of God. Since that day, every man has been desperately trying to prove that he is the Unique One to his parents, his peers, his enemies, his children, his wife, and most of all, himself. However, created beings can only receive validation from their Creator. Only the One may validate a man as having achieved equality with God. Unfortunately, the Unique One will never validate anyone as a successful replication.

Few men would dare to proclaim that their principal purpose in life is to achieve equality with God and, ultimately, superiority over God. We remain tight-lipped about our true intent to keep everyone guessing. We prefer veiling our narcissism in nobility, and toward this end, men employ many differing taking-tactics. Some men proclaim that all they desire is to be the most loved. Others that they merely desire to be the most respected. Still more yearn only to be the most revered. However, there is only One who is the most loved, respected, and revered. Even men who humbly proclaim that all they desire is to be a good man are hoping that no one points out that there is only one who is Good. In the end, every fallen man has only one desire—to be like God.

Since every man's sole ambition is to become like, gain position over, and ultimately dethrone God, men should not be surprised to find themselves plagued by an innate sense of failure. Still, we do find a perverse sense of validation through competition. Men compete against one another, fight one another, and kill one another amidst the hope of crushing underfoot all who bear the likeness of the Masculine One. Then, once a man believes he has accumulated enough masculine corpses beneath his feet, he'll feel sufficiently confident to challenge God for supremacy over everything and everyone.

Each masculine spectacle of competition is an exhibition match designed to prepare a man to call out, battle with, and ultimately defeat God. Men naively believe that defeating other masculine ones will validate them as the Masculine One. As fallen beings, we each naively believe we're competing with one another over the position of Success. However, what we're actually doing is competing with one another over who is the greatest of the failures.

The One, who is unlike anyone, cannot compete. Being unique makes God categorically incomparable to any other. Conversely, fallen men can and do compete against one another because we're all the lesser replicas of the first one who desired to be like the One. Consequently, untouched souls waste their entire existence conforming to self-fabricated conceptions of Perfection, completely unaware that the Perfect One cannot be replicated. Fallen men desire to take God's world, God's position, and God's identity. Like God's enemy, a fallen man will never rest until he has it all, so he alone can be the One over all.

As each man competes with every other man over who is the greatest of the failures, we're all unwittingly heralding our doom. Feminine creation—and the women who embody her likeness—live to express the Masculine One and each of His masculine ones. What each feminine partner wants is a masculine partner who uniquely portrays the Masculine Partner. Therefore, the more aggressively a man competes with other men to present himself as the Unique One, the more acutely our orchestrational mother and every nearby woman will spiritually know, inwardly sense, and materially express his failure to be Unique.

If a man's problem is simply material failure, then all he needs to do is think, feel, and act differently. However, if a man's problem is being a spiritual failure, then the solution is beyond his grasp. Failing is a material problem. Being a failure is a spiritual problem. Every man fails materially because his lightless, loveless, and lifeless soul is a failure.

The male body that does not contain a living spiritual being of unique world-making authority within his soul is a spiritual failure destined to produce an endless string of material failures to robustly express the unalterable truth. Consequently, the solution to a man's failure to be unique is not to replicate the Unique One. Instead, the solution is to submit his soul to the One who is unlike anyone so he might receive the inseminating touch that will make him, also, unlike anyone.

The material dependencies that fallen men grow increasingly addicted to shame their masculine likeness. Depending upon wealth, women, or glory to make one unique can only lead to one end. Yet, the material vices that each man grows increasingly dependent upon will always remain good. What is not good is depending upon even one atom of material creation for one's spiritual ascension into Perfection.

Everything a fallen man touches will obediently express him as one who has failed to be Unique. The apparent malice of creation—that every man curses—is actually her sacrificial service. Creation wishes to help every man mentally perceive, emotionally feel, and physically experience the futility of trying to make a unique world within her without first being touched by the Unique One. The masculine life debt to toil, suffer, and fail amidst God's world is creation's gift to compel each man to consensually bow before the Masculine One.

A man's desire to be like God is the noble veneer masking the depraved depths of his fallen narcissism. After all, only one can be the One. Therefore, replacing God is the sole purpose of every fallen man. Originally, God gave the first man material authority over creation so he might ensure the world-making opportunity of every soul touched by God. Presently, fallen men use their body's authoritative likeness in a futile attempt to make themselves into the Authority. Fallen men fight, ruin, and destroy everything in their quest to be the one who rules, fills, and subdues all. The great tragedy of fallen masculinity is that while each strives toward becoming more and more like God, each is becoming less and less like a man.

Facing one's failure to be Unique is what leads a man back to Success. Masculinity requires being a unique one. Fallen ones want to replicate the Unique One, while the Unique One wants to make each one unlike anyone. Being a unique one—who is unlike anyone—is the polar opposite of being like the Unique One. God's enemy desires to conform all into his likeness to validate himself as the Perfect One. Conversely, the Perfect One desires to make everyone into one who is unlike anyone, which demands that He ensures that no one becomes like Him.

A fallen man wastes his entire life trying to be like the Unique One, unaware that if he succeeds, he'll become an exact replica of God, thereby eliminating his uniqueness and God's uniqueness simultaneously. Only God is Unique. And only God can make each one into a unique one. The man seeking to be like God is just like every other man, while the man who surrenders his soul to God will awaken into one who is unlike anyone—especially unlike God. Then, a resurrected man may begin leading all toward the One who can give them their own likeness of His uniqueness so that each might begin making their own unique world within God's world of unique worlds.

Unfortunately, accepting one's failure to be like God is not a solution, despite it being the only option. All human solutions are worthless, including accepting one's own worthlessness. The only solution for an untouched soul of infinite emptiness is to return, amidst the present moment of our timeless spiritual existence, to submissive dependence upon Infinite Fullness.

When the Masculine Creator entered the material realm, He neither exalted nor degraded His masculinity. Instead, He spiritually, inwardly, and materially displayed His uniqueness while leading everyone to the One who could make them unlike anyone, which, of course, was Him. Likewise, a masculine creator lives his life neither as Success nor as a worthless failure. Instead, a resurrected man is merely one who has accepted his failure to be the Unique One and is now growing into a unique one. Then, such a man may begin leading everyone to the One capable of giving them their own likeness of His uniqueness.

A man spiritually touched by God will think, feel, and act unlike anyone. Still, facing and embracing one's failure to be like God is not a decision made by the mind, a sensation engendered by the heart, or action taken by the body. Uniqueness is what defines masculinity and becoming a unique one requires the moment-by-moment surrender of one's soul without contemplation, without consideration, and without condition to the touch of the Unique One.

Chapter 5
Leading Amidst Death and Dust

A man's original responsibility as the material embodiment of the Masculine Creator was to ensure the survival, comfort, and orchestration of every world maker and their world amidst God's world. Since God had a vested interest in each man who would be materially representing His masculinity, He intentionally placed the first man into a position of material authority without equal or oversight. However, the first man gave away his position of material authority in a fool-hearted attempt to become the spiritual Authority. Now, each man spiritually separate from God leads humanity as one who is nothing, nowhere, and no one, culminating in everyone's death and a swift return to the dust.

Fallen men are no longer material authorities without equal or oversight. The first man gave each man's rightful position to the taker in an attempt to become the World Maker. Still, every male body continues to retain its material likeness of Authority. As a result, an irreconcilable incongruence exists between a man's material embodiment of Authority and his spiritual soul who has never known the touch of Authority.

Although the first man abandoned his responsibility before God, God did not abandon humanity. Instead, God became a man to become the Man so He might reclaim the first man's original position of material authority over creation without equal or oversight. Then, the Man left the material realm so that each soul might make their own decision to either return to Him to become a unique authority or continue in their doomed effort to become the Authority.

Today, only the Man holds the first man's position as the material authority over creation without equal or oversight, allowing any man who desires to return to that position by first approaching the Man. Then, each spiritually submissive man may receive the Man's touch upon his soul to be awakened into a unique spiritual being capable of wielding the first man's original position of material authority so the newly resurrected unique one might begin his personal growth as a masculine creator.

God's touch upon a submissive soul gives humanity that which matters most for world-making: an independent, authoritative, and unique spiritual being. Only then may a man begin living as a masculine creator who is serving the survival, comfort, and orchestrational success of all. Consequently, the man who gives his life—which is already doomed to toil, suffering, and failure—to preserve those God loves will be treasured by all and the One who loves all. As a result, each man must decide if he will expend his doomed life for himself, for others, or in the service of the One who loves him and all others.

God gave the first man a position of authority without equal or oversight so he might ensure that no one gets into a position of authority over anyone. God wants each unique one completely free to express who He's made them to be by creating their own unique world within His world. The male body is the blunt instrument of forceful, aggressive violence designed to protect the sovereign world-making authority of every soul from any outside-in encroachment, violation, or invasion.

God formed His world to materially mother each unique one that He spiritually fathered. Since the material body housing our soul is an integral aspect of creation, we owe her our gentleness, appreciation, and love as our material matriarch. Even amidst the present fallen age of darkness, decay, and death, a man must lead humanity to respect creation for her service in so vividly expressing our lifeless spiritual nature. The man who reveres God, respects creation, and recognizes every human creator is one who is leading all back toward being a race world of unique world makers who, together, will make a world of unique worlds.

The toil, suffering, and failure each man experiences flow to him from the first man. As a result, each man who aspires to return to the abandoned position of the first man must shoulder holistic responsibility for our entire species. Only a man who does not shirk the consequences that flow from the first man will return in desperation to the Man to be made into a masculine creator. Any man who embraces anything less than holistic responsibility for our entire species will be just another man blaming all other men as the means to validate himself as the one and only true Man.

Our spiritual nature comes from the Creator, and our material nature comes from creation. Each human soul exists in God's spiritual realm, and each human body exists in creation's material realm so that each human being might link those two realms together through their inner realm. Consequently, God designed humanity to fulfill his desire to continue His original world-making union with creation through each human being. Likewise, creation wants to continue her original world-making union with her Creator alongside each human being. We, as God's race of unique world makers, are the triune link that allows the original world-making partnership to continue making world makers who will each make their own unique world within God's world.

Amidst our inner realm, we create a never-before-seen mental, emotional, and physical likeness of the spiritually unique one that God has already conceived from within our souls. Our Creator leads our soul. Our soul leads our mind, heart, and body. And our mind, heart, and body lead creation. A man exists to ensure that each human being's world-making partnership remains securely anchored to the Creator in the spiritual realm and to creation in the material realm, which is the masculine task that the first man failed, the Man succeeded, and any man of faith now returns.

Without God implanting our souls with our own likeness of His uniqueness, we'll remain nothing, nowhere, and no one. Without creation enveloping our soul in a material body customized to our uniqueness, we'll remain unable to express the spiritual something, somewhere, and someone we're becoming. However, without us expressing our likeness of Uniqueness out into creation—through our mind, heart, and body—she'll remain unable to become the world of unique worlds that she desires. Only together as spiritual Father, material mother, and world-making children will everyone find fulfillment for their foremost desire.

When we consider the triune design of humanity, it becomes clear that the spiritual realm is under God's authority, and the material realm is under creation's authority. However, the inner realm—which binds together God's spiritual realm and creation's material realm—is under our authority. Since each realm is overseen by God, creation, or human creators, cultivating mutually beneficial partnerships between everyone is essential. Orchestrating a world of unique worlds depends upon everyone fulfilling what they desire in a way that allows everyone else to fulfill what they desire. A man is the authority bearing both a spiritual position before the Creator and a material position before creation designed to lead all humanity amidst the original world-making partnership between the Creator, creation, and every human creator.

A man's central position within the original world-making partnership is reclaimed the moment he surrenders his soul back to God. Then, the Creator's spiritual authority may flow through the man's soul, into his inner realm, and out into his personal portion of creation's material realm to bind all three realms together into one. The triune realms of God's original world-making design are held together by each man who lives with Him in the spiritual realm, with his mind, heart, and body in his inner realm and with creation in her material realm.

Nothing lasts. All bodies die because all souls are born spiritually separate from the One who is Light, Love, and Life. Even if we return our souls to God, the end for our material bodies is already set based on our spiritual beginning. Therefore, every atom that comprises every fallen creator's body and their world will eventually crumble back into the dust. However, any spiritually unique one awakened by God's touch shall persist through their bond of faith to the Eternal Arc, who will ferry their soul through the approaching collapse of taker's present age and deliver them into the Maker's coming age. Therefore, the man who recognizes God's desire for unique ones and expends his doomed life to protect, preserve, and procure those most treasured by God will defiantly lead humanity through the present age of death and dust and on into the age of creators yet to come.

Chapter 6
The Duty of a Doomed Man

Everything that a lifeless, spiritual void touches will immediately begin crumbling toward darkness, decay, and death. Creation's material atoms can do nothing but express spiritual beings. A masculine creator takes it upon himself to lead humanity to respect our mother's sacrificial service, despite that sacrificial service also condemning his own body and world to die. The duty of a doomed man is to embrace his failure to be the Unique One, return to the Unique One, and then lead humanity to revere God, respect creation, and recognize every human creator.

Every soul begins as a spiritual void of infinite emptiness. We're all nothing, nowhere, and no one without God's spiritual insemination. Each who is spiritually separate from God will pursue perfect replication, which inhibits them from attaining any unique orchestration. As fallen beings, we avoid pursuing uniqueness because doing so would result in us having to face our failure to be like the Unique One. Sadly, the longer we resist God's touch in our effort to become like God, without God, the longer each will remain a non-existent replication of Perfection, just like everyone else.

When God touches our souls, He conceives a new creation from within our void-like spiritual wombs who is unlike anyone. The only thing God expects from each unique one is to remain spiritually dependent upon Him so that He might continue making them even more unique. Then, the more spiritually unique we become, the more emphatically material creation will strive toward expressing our uniqueness.

Our spiritual Father delights in making unique world makers. Our material mother delights in making unique worlds. And each human being delights in being made into a unique world maker so they might make their own unique world. Only together, amidst the original orchestrational partnership, do we all find fulfillment.

The man who reveres the Creator, respects creation, and recognizes every human creator will expend his doomed life to lead all back toward the original world-making partnership. Each masculine creator must lead humanity through the toil, suffering, and failure we've created back toward our original position in between the arms of our spiritual Father and our material mother. Consequently, any man who expends the remainder of his doomed days leading a race of replicated world takers back toward being a race of unique world makers is one that the Unique One will want leading His people and His world amidst the coming age of creators.

God responded to the first man's choice by obligating His world to obstruct everyone's efforts to become like Him. Presently, creation is our incubation chamber, retaining our lifeless souls and sustaining our faltering bodies while prohibiting us from accessing the fullness of her orchestrational potential. As fallen beings, we're each alive materially but dead spiritually. However, each soul is merely a dormant, void-like embryo awaiting the spiritually inseminating touch of the Unique One.

A masculine creator pushes everyone toward God to ensure each has their chance to return to the Unique One and become one of His unique ones. Then, a man may work to ensure the material survival, comfort, and orchestration of every world maker being made by the World Maker. What the Masculine Creator works to provide to each spiritual soul, a masculine creator works to provide to each material body.

A man exists to use his masculine strength, position, and authority to forcefully keep everyone from getting into a position of authority over anyone. As fallen beings, we're all presently assaulting one another's sovereignty, individuality, and liberty in a doomed effort to

46

present ourselves as the One destined to rule, fill, and subdue all. Since every untouched soul wants to be like God, a masculine creator is the single greatest obstacle to everyone's desire to seize control over everything and everyone so they alone can be the One. Therefore, a man authoritatively intervenes between all to protect the sovereignty, individuality, and liberty of all so that each one might retain their opportunity to become a unique one and make their own unique world.

Our material mother looks expectantly to each man to protect God's unique ones so all might remain free from any form of servility, conformity, or tyranny. Mother Nature wants everyone to enjoy their own unrestricted sovereignty, individuality, and liberty amidst her atoms so each might make their personal portion of her into their own unique world, so she might become God's world of unique worlds. The Creator's curse already obligates creation to obstruct everyone attempting to be the One. Therefore, a man who returns to leading mankind must partner with Mother Nature by also keeping anyone from getting into a position of authority over anyone so each might exert their own world-making likeness, from the inside out, free from any outside-in meddling.

The only way a man can hope to repulse the spiritual corruption spreading outward from the surface of every tainted soul is to ceaselessly submit his own soul to God. Then, having experienced how the Authoritative One deals with his nature as a taker, a man will start to see, feel, and experience how he might do likewise for his own mind, heart, and body. Only after a man has begun authoritatively obstructing himself from corrupting his own inner realm should he attempt to join creation in obstructing humanity from corrupting her material realm.

Everyone's taking-tactics rise from the surface of their tainted soul before infesting their mind, infecting their heart, and corrupting their body with the desire to invade creation. However, a man can push the entire taking process backward through the body, heart, and mind of

47

a fallen being and toward the tainted soul from which it all came. The more skillfully and forcefully a man exerts his masculine push, the more efficiently and effectively he may protect creation and human creators from the spiritual nature of the taker that we each bear.

The more aggressively, intimately, and repetitiously an untouched soul touches creation's atoms, the more robustly Mother Nature is obligated to express their lightless, loveless, and lifeless soul. Although a masculine creator cannot stop humanity from ultimately turning creation into a calamity, he can stop individual efforts from going unchallenged. No man can undo the corruption allowed by the first man. However, any man can follow the example of the Man by forcefully pushing back against the desire that is rising from within everyone to be the One.

A masculine creator leads mankind back toward the lost age of world makers, amidst the present age as world takers, in preparation for the age of creators yet to come. Each man desires, is designed, and is expected to lead our species forward. A man who knows he is not the One, and spiritually bows before the One—to become a unique one— will lead all toward Uniqueness.

A masculine creator shows no mercy to anyone's taking-tactics, starting with his own. Although no man can alter the spiritual likeness of any soul any man who embodies the Masculine One may push back against the mental, emotional, and physical taking-tactics of all. As a result, any attempt to encroach, violate, or invade any world maker's world will arouse the wrath of a masculine creator just as it does in the Masculine Creator.

A resurrected man can trace the material darkness, decay, and death that creation is obediently expressing backward through everyone's mind, heart, and body and straight into their tainted spiritual soul. The duty of a doomed man is to embrace the unalterable truth of humanity's failure, of which he is responsible. Then, as he shoulders his masculine life debt, a man may lead humanity forward amidst the consequences of our corruption by protecting, preserving, and procuring the one thing of eternal value left in the present fallen age: each unique one conceived by the Unique One.

Section 3
The Determined Man

A man's determination is measured by how unabashedly, unhesitantly, and unmercifully he exerts aggressive masculine force. Fallen men use their repulsive nature to push everyone toward destruction since their intent is to remove anyone obstructing them from becoming the One. Resurrected men—who wield an even greater capacity for destruction as those who are being touched, shaped, and breathed into by the Destroyer—will turn their ever-expanding destructive capacity upon anyone or anything, maintaining humanity's dependence upon material creation. As a result, a masculine creator frees humanity from material bondage by forcefully imparting his own touch of independence so that each might orchestrate their own world as a self-defining, self-governing, and self-determining sovereign being.

52

Chapter 7
Seeing the Sovereign Spheres

A fallen man sees only one world—God's world as his world. A resurrected man sees a plethora of worlds alongside his world, which are each being held together by mutually beneficial partnerships within God's one world of unique worlds. Seeing every world within God's world is what allows a man to exert his aggressive masculine nature to the benefit of all. Consequently, the sovereignty of each soul is what a man uses his strength, position, and authority to protect. Anyone attempting to encroach upon the sovereign domain of another must be forcibly repulsed. Anyone attempting to violate the sovereign body of another must be violently removed. And anyone attempting to invade the sovereign soul of another must be mercilessly destroyed.

The man spiritually touched by God knows the Creator's love for every soul, body, and world. A man is the conduit designed to conduct the Creator's zeal for those He loves from the spiritual realm, through the inner realm, and into the material realm. However, merely conducting the Creator's passion for protecting every soul, body, and world is not enough. The infinite and zealous nature of God's love needs to be scaled down and focused into a force that will benefit all. Therefore, a man must design his inner realm to help him mentally see each world, emotionally feel each world, and physically protect each world with a suitable portion of God's fury.

Seeing humanity's sovereign spheres begins in the mind. Each soul touched by God becomes one who can authoritatively direct their mind toward cognitively depicting everyone's world-making authority. Therefore, a masculine creator leads his mind to sketch an illuminated sphere around every human being to mark the outer periphery of their world-making authority within God's world. Then, a man's spiritual being may look out through his mind's work to see a spherical demarcation for every world maker's world. As a result, a masculine creator will be able to perceive the mobile spheres of personal sovereignty that he must not violate and prohibit others from violating.

A human creator's world comprises three elements: their soul, their body, and the material objects they're presently utilizing to make their world. As a result, a man's mind may mentally illuminate a sphere centered upon each soul that encompasses their body and their material possessions. However, a sovereign's sphere is not static. Everything in creation is always ebbing, flowing, and growing. For example, when we enter our home, our sovereign sphere expands to encompass all the material objects we own. However, when we enter a crowded street, our sovereign sphere contracts to avoid encroaching upon the sovereignty of others. A man's mental depiction of each creator's world-making authority is a tool to reveal for him the outer periphery of each creator's personal domain amidst the ever-changing complexities of God's fluid, flexible, and feminine world.

Each sovereign's sphere encapsulates their triune existence as a spiritual, inner, and material world maker. Every world maker exists in the spiritual realm under God's authority, in their inner realm under their own authority, and in the material realm under creation's authority. Each spiritual sovereign conceived by the Authority radiates their own authority out from their soul, through their inner realm, and into their personal portion of creation's material realm. Still, as finite beings, no one gets to rule, fill, and subdue all. Therefore, the man who mentally perceives each sovereign's domain—as a single illuminated sphere around their body—will find himself able to exert his forceful masculine nature in a way that leads a race of replicated world takers back toward being a race of unique world makers.

No man's mind intuitively perceives a sphere of sovereignty around any soul because he's born perceiving himself as the Sovereign. However, once a man mentally depicts his own sovereign sphere radiating out from within his soul and encompassing his mind, heart, body, and material possessions, then he's clearly marked a limit to his own authority. Until a man consciously limits his own authority within God's world, he'll remain just like every other fallen man who is unwittingly encroaching, violating, and invading the sovereignty of all.

The greatest threat to the sovereignty of every soul is a man who sees no limit to his own authority within God's world. Fallen men see only external obstructions that are challenging their perceived right to globally dominate everything and everyone. However, a resurrected man willfully erects a mental sphere of sovereignty around himself to depict the limit of his own authority. Then, a man may begin wielding his repulsive masculine nature to protect the sovereignty of everyone without violating the sovereignty of anyone.

Mentally depicting everyone's sovereign sphere will not stop takers from taking. However, seeing a conceptual depiction of every world maker's world will provide a masculine mind, heart, and body with a tool to guide them toward mentally, emotionally, and physically obstructing everyone's taking-tactics. Each man's mind wants to craft an illuminated sphere around every soul to demarcate each sovereign's mobile domain of world-making authority within God's world. Once this mental effort is underway, a man will find his heart awakening amidst its desire to fill each sovereign sphere with the potent emotions needed to activate his body's protective actions.

God treasures the sovereignty of every soul so much that He decided to restrict Himself from directly intervening in the material realm. Maintaining the sovereignty of every self-defining, self-governing, and self-determining soul is essential in God's eyes, which is why He created the male body. A man is a finite, scaled-down version of the Masculine Creator. God's sphere of sovereignty is infinite, making His physical presence the single greatest threat to everyone's world-making authority. Originally, our Creator's plan was to walk beside each world maker in the spiritual realm so that His omnipresent authority would not threaten anyone's sovereignty in the material realm. Then, God made the first man to ensure humanity and creation would not go without a finite representation of His masculine protection.

A mental image is a container for emotions. When a man's mind depicts any object—such as a sovereign sphere of world-making authority around every soul—his heart will naturally swell with passion to emotionally fill each of those cognitive containers. The protective emotions available to a man are wide-ranging: from wrath to warmth, from chaos to calm, and from brutality to tranquility. The more emotions a man's heart prepares ahead of time, the better. Reacting swiftly, rationally, and effectively to the varied forms of infringement upon the sovereignty of others requires pre-formed emotions filling a man's mental depiction of every sovereign's sphere.

A man's heart desires to create and pour forth a complex concoction of emotions into each sphere of sovereignty depicted by his mind. Then, his actions will have a deep reserve of meaningful emotions to draw upon. A masculine creator cannot only have one emotion for protection. He needs a deep emotional reservoir to unleash actions suitable for unintentional encroachments, deceptive violations, and aggressive invasions. Once each sphere of sovereignty depicted within a man's mind is pressurized with his potently protective emotions, then anyone foolish enough to puncture the outer periphery of any world under a man's protection will be swept away by the zealous torrent of his repulsive actions.

The most frightening material force in existence is a male body flush with emotion and fixated on punishing a perceived violation. Unfortunately, fallen men direct their destructive capacity toward destroying anyone encroaching, violating, or invading their world, which they naively perceive as the entirety of God's world. Tainted souls see no lines demarcating any limits to their personal authority. A fallen man sees himself as the Sovereign, thereby fully justifying him in destroying anyone who missteps within his universal domain. Conversely, a resurrected man directs the same capacity for mental, emotional, and physical destruction but toward protecting the sovereignty sphere of every single soul. As a man grows into a masculine creator, he'll progressively marvel at how fluidly God's world submissively serves the authority of every human being. Depicting everyone's sovereign sphere and filling each with the emotions he needs to animate his body's protective actions is an indispensable step for any man who intends to lead humanity back toward being a race of unique world makers.

Creation both seeks and fears masculine creators. The entire universal whole of our orchestrational mother still longs for the touch of any man who has returned to the position of the first man. However, our material mother also harbors deep-seated bitterness toward all men after dealing with so many presenting themselves as the promised leader of mankind. As a result, even a resurrected masculine creator who diligently protects the sovereignty of every soul for the remainder of his days will not win over our embittered material matriarch. Still, a man may prepare himself as the protector of every soul's sovereignty in the present age in preparation for doing likewise in the age of creators yet to come.

Where there are mental illuminations and flowing emotions, there will be fiery actions. What the mind sees, and the heart feels will cause the body to act. Therefore, a man leading his mind to see, his heart to feel, and his body to act as the protector of every sovereign's sphere is a masculine creator who is bearing and exerting his own unique likeness of the Masculine Creator. Then, as a man progressively begins to protect the sovereignty of every soul, he'll begin leading each world maker toward making their own unique world as he authoritatively, forcefully, and aggressively ensures that each one is the only one ruling, filling, and subduing their personal and mobile portion of Mother Nature.

Chapter 8
Destroying Dependence

God is the Destroyer, and He made the male body in His likeness to be a destroyer. Consequently, the soul touched by the Destroyer—who also bears the body of a destroyer—will exert destruction. No man can stop his body from doing what it was designed to do. However, what a man can do is exert his masculine destruction in a way that protects all creation and every creator.

What gets the Masculine Creator upset is any soul depending upon anything or anyone other than Him. Ever since the first man and woman consumed the forbidden material fruit—which they hoped would make them like God—every ensuing thought, emotion, and action from humanity has been expanded our race's ever-increasing dependence upon creation. Therefore, the man who destroys mankind's dependence upon our material mother will increase the opportunity for each untouched soul to consensually return to dependence upon our spiritual Father.

God is presently restraining Himself from directly interfering in the material realm so that He might not infringe upon the sovereignty of any soul. As the Destroyer, God obliterates anything and anyone not dependent upon Him. Therefore, to protect creation and give each self-defining, self-governing, and self-determining soul their chance at returning to Him as their Creator, God is restraining Himself from destroying humanity's material dependence. Instead, He looks expectantly to those who bear His masculine likeness amidst His hope that each man might exert his own scaled-down version of the Destroyer.

Masculinity is destructive because it separates creators from creation. Amidst the orbital nature of our orchestrational mother, a man's linear repulsion cuts across creation's circular patterns to interrupt her natural processes and carve out sovereign spheres distinctly separate from her universal whole. A man is ideally suited to demarcate the boundaries of each sovereign's unique world as it exists independent from, interconnected with, and interdependent on God's world of unique worlds. Although each creator's world must remain linked to God's world, a masculine creator must work tirelessly to cut away each spiritual creator from growing dependent upon material creation.

During the first seven days, God demonstrated His masculinity by cutting across creation's universal whole to form visionary, meaningful, and purposeful separations. However, the Creator enacted each repulsive separation for the purpose of ensuring His principal purpose—making a world that would help Him make unique world makers. Similarly, a man wields his linear nature by cutting lines demarcating each sovereign's world within God's world. Our material mother will obediently recognize and respect a man's authoritative separations, but only if she senses him leading her toward becoming God's world of unique worlds and not his world of unique worlds.

No man can force another to return to spiritual dependence upon our Father. However, any man can destroy anyone's material dependence upon our mother. A masculine creator draws a line across creation's anatomical currents to lead each toward mentally seeing, emotionally feeling, and physically respecting their sovereign domain and everyone else's sovereign domain. Seeing, feeling, and experiencing everyone's sovereign sphere will also begin exposing the taking-tactics we're all employing to make others materially dependent upon us.

The last thing we want is the Creator, creation, and other human creators growing aware of the tactics we're employing to take control of every soul, every body, and every world, within God's world. We each coax those around us toward materially depending upon objects that we control in the material realm because it makes them susceptible to our external influence. Once a soul is dependent upon an object we control, then moving that object will also move the soul. Externally controlling another is only possible if they're first willfully dependent upon something we control in the material realm. Therefore, a masculine creator lives to destroy everyone's dependence upon every material thing to ensure that no world-making sovereign unwittingly gets themselves into a position where their world, their body, or their soul is being controlled by another.

The male body wants to exert linear destruction. First, a man carves up God's world into a world of unique worlds. Then, he pushes back against each one who is attempting to cross the lines of sovereignty he's laid to keep everyone from invading anyone else's world. Finally, a man will work tirelessly to cut each soul off from growing dependent upon any material thing. The Creator and creation will support a masculine creator's destructive efforts, but only if he is leading all toward dependence upon our Father and independence from our mother.

Cutting spheres of sovereignty into creation is what allows a man to see anyone who is encroaching, violating, or invading the authority of another. Then, like a master swordsman, a man's linear nature may sweep out along the outer periphery of a sovereign domain to cut away any mental, emotional, or physical taking-tactics, regardless of whether they are trying to get into or get out of a creator's world. Even souls who have returned to God's touch will still need the sharpened edge of masculine repulsion to continually cut down the taking-tactics they're unconsciously employing against everyone around them.

Destroying humanity's material dependence requires employing a customized approach to everyone who is attempting to be like the One. However, a basic principle is to always exert a destructive force that is just one magnitude higher than the taking-tactic being employed. For example, anyone gazing longingly at a material object inside another creator's world might receive a menacing glare from a masculine creator. If they ignore a man's warning glare by reaching for the object they desire, then a masculine creator might slap their outstretched hand. Should they ignore a man's glare and slap by lunging for the object they desire, a masculine creator will be forced to sieze control of their body and physically remove them from the sovereign domain of another.

A male body needs to see the linear periphery of each world maker's world. Without these lines, a man's destructive exertions will prove feeble and erratic in his attempts to protect the sovereignty of every soul. The complexities inherent to knowing what type and magnitude of force to exert in protecting every sovereign's sphere will develop over time. However, the foundation for all a man's destructive separations is to preserve the sovereignty of every soul, and their world, from the taking-tactics of all.

Human minds, hearts, or bodies are not the problem. Rather, it is the souls leading human minds, hearts, and bodies that are the problem. A man uses his repulsive mind, heart, and body to communicate with a taker's soul through their mind, heart, and body. However, a man must be careful to unleash his masculine forms of repulsive protection in a manner that minimizes the damage to everyone's material nature. Each human form is precious to creation and to the Creator. Damaging the mind, heart, and body of another is a last resort. Only when a soul has fully corrupted their mind, heart, and body with an unrestricted, unrestrained, and unalterable drive to take should a man utilize force sufficient to permanently separate a soul from a body.

Allowing any soul to increase their dependence upon creation inhibits them from returning to the Creator. A soul of infinite emptiness who is depending upon finite material creation for sustenance will never have enough. As a result, any soul a man is obstructing from consuming creation will begin to starve, spiritually. The purpose of this intentional spiritual starvation is to awaken the true depths of another's void and leave them with only the One as an option for satiation. Only when a soul is physically forced to face the eternal state awaiting them the moment their body dies will anyone consciously consider returning to feast exclusively upon the spiritual One.

Any soul dependent upon any material object is enslaved to the one who controls that material object. Since every fallen soul is currently born one hundred percent dependent upon material creation, we're all presently enslaved to anyone who moves anything. A masculine creator lives to forcefully detach every soul from their dependence upon our material mother. Each male is born innately wanting what our Father wants—a race of independent, authoritative, and unique world makers.

Similar to how a woman has no respect for a man who worships her, so creation has no respect for a world maker who depends upon her. A man goes forth to authoritatively, forcefully, and aggressively obstruct anyone who is trying to increase humanity's dependence upon anything or anyone other than the One. God values the man who destroys humanity's material dependence. Creation as well looks affectionately upon the man who is exerting visionary, meaningful, and purposeful separations through her atoms to ensure each one becomes a unique world maker. However, fallen beings will not take kindly to a man who is obstructing them from consuming every atom and controlling every soul. Still, a masculine creator's destructive excursions will always serve the deepest desires of the Creator, creation, and every human creator by forcefully pushing everyone toward the One who will make them into a unique one, destined to make their own unique world within God's world of unique worlds.

Chapter 9
The Touch of Independence

A masculine creator destroys humanity's dependence upon material creation so that each soul might have the opportunity to return to depending exclusively upon the spiritual Creator. Ever since mankind first took and ate from the forbidden material tree, every soul has been increasing their consumptive dependency upon Mother Nature. Therefore, a masculine creator patrols the sovereign spheres of humanity so he might systematically obstruct everyone who is attempting to take from anyone. However, at the center of each sovereign's sphere is the greatest threat of all. As a result, a masculine creator exerts a touch of independence that pushes each world maker back from consuming even their own world to force them toward the Maker of the world.

The best way to keep a taker from invading anyone else's world is to keep them inside their own world. Unfortunately, every untouched soul's desire for spiritual Light, Love, and Life is infinite, compelling them to drain every anatomical object within their grasp. As timeless, spaceless, and matterless spiritual voids, our appetite for material consumption is limitless. Therefore, even if a man keeps fallen souls inside their own world, he will not stop them from consuming creation, which will continue increasing their material dependence upon our mother and their spiritual independence from our Father.

Every creator's world eventually implodes due to the draining effect of the void within. Each soul sensing this impending disaster concludes that the only way to sustain themselves and their world is to expand the scope of their material consumption. Unfortunately, since every soul is an infinite void of spiritual emptiness, allowing anyone to expand the scope of their consumption across creation's finite material realm will only increase the number of atoms being drained. Consequently, a masculine creator intervenes on the behalf of creation by pushing everyone back from consuming any world, including their own. A man's repulsive touch compounds every soul's spiritual starvation so all might be forced to live materially independent from creation, leaving each with only One option for spiritual satiation.

A masculine creator is not precisely protecting creation from fallen creators. Instead, a masculine creator is actually protecting fallen creators from creation. As spiritual beings, we're each privileged guests amidst our mother's material realm. Creation innately recognizes each soul as potentially a unique one capable of making one of the unique worlds that she needs to become God's world of unique worlds, which initially garners us each significant trust, respect, and leeway. As our mother experiences our abhorrent orchestrational incompetence, she simply assumes we need more time beneath the World Maker's touch to ennoble us into a more independent, authoritative, and unique world maker. However, as our years of orchestrational incompetence stretch out into decades, our mother will begin to sense that something far more troubling is at play.

As untouched souls of infinite spiritual emptiness, our only hope for satiation is to ceaselessly take and consume each of creation's material expressions of Light, Love, and Life in the hope that doing so will somehow conceive from within our soul one who is a replication of Light, Love, and Life. Fallen beings desire to consume everything, control everywhere, and command everyone. However, creation cannot allow anyone to dominate her holistically because she exists to enable everyone to make their own unique world within her, so she might become God's world of unique worlds. As a result, every soul intent on consuming everything and dominating everyone eventually gets spewed out by creation, thereby eternally affixing them as an untouched void of infinite emptiness with no Creator and no creation upon which to feast.

Creation is presently using the finite nature of our material bodies to restrict the infinite spiritual craving she senses within us. The human form may only direct so many atoms toward our spiritual void at any one time. Additionally, since each human body remains an integral aspect of material creation, the more we materially consume, the more we communicate to creation what we ultimately intend. Amidst this ever-increasing danger, a man may forcefully impose material independence by halting anyone's taking-tactics to intentionally accelerate their spiritual starvation. The spiritual starvation a man induces will then protect a soul from further arousing our mother's wrath. As a result, enforcing material independence upon everyone buys humanity a little more time for a few more souls to exist within creation in the hope that they, too, might return to spiritually depending upon, and consuming, only the Creator.

A masculine creator who enforces material independence will engender hatred from every fallen one. No one takes kindly to having their hand perpetually slapped away from the next choice cluster of atoms that they're sure will finally engender their ascension into Perfection. After all, a taker believes that they are the rightful ruler, filler, and subduer of all. Denying them their right to consume what they already view as wholly theirs will enrage them. Therefore, a man must make sure his forceful touch resonates with the authoritative expectation that every spiritual being in his presence, beginning with himself, will exist independent from everything and everyone other than the One.

Fallen beings cannot comprehend how futile it is to attempt to become a unique one by replicating the Unique One. The first fallen being, after an unknown number of millennia, is still unaware of this truth. In contrast, a masculine creator knows with zealous certainty that no one who is trying to be like anyone will become a unique one.

Furthermore, consuming material objects that express the Unique One is also no way to engender uniqueness. Therefore, the man who forcefully, aggressively, and destructively ensures everyone is spiritually starving is demonstrating, demanding, and determining how every soul in his presence will live independently from creation.

Every soul craves material creation because she still resonates with the Creator's touch. However, the moment we stuff our mother's anatomical treasures into our bodies and toward our souls, we always find ourselves unsatisfied. Worse yet, having tasted a few choice morsels of our material mother's light, love, and life only further awakens our insatiable appetite for Light, Love, and Life. Therefore, when a masculine creator intercedes by forcefully inducing material independence, he's decided that a soul has consumed enough of material creation to awaken their desire for the Creator and is now ready to burn in the endless agony of their infinite spiritual emptiness for Infinite Fullness.

A masculine creator forces everyone to grow independent from creation so that all might burn together as lightless, loveless, and lifeless souls. Although condemning all to burn in spiritual agony appears brutal, doing so is proper, just, and necessary. The first man chose to lead humanity toward creation and away from the Creator. Then, the Man came to lead humanity away from creation and back toward the Creator. Now, each man must choose where his touch will lead our species.

Denying a soul material sustenance so they might burn in the endless agony of their unquenchable spiritual desire is a merciless affair. Fortunately, a man is the custom-designed blunt object of forceful aggression needed to deny humanity's lesser aims in the service of humanity's greatest aim. The most merciful thing a man can do is to force every soul in his presence to burn amidst their self-inflicted state of infinite spiritual emptiness, leaving them no option other than returning to Infinite Fullness before it's too late.

Independent choice is what got us into our present fallen mess. At the same time, independent choice is also what gives us hope. However, we do not actually have the choice of independence. Instead, mankind only has a choice of dependence. The taker deceived humanity into believing we could choose independence from God by cleverly getting us to choose dependence upon creation. The key is in understanding that we had to eat the forbidden material fruit before we achieved our spiritual independence from God. Making our souls materially dependent upon our mother is what made us spiritually independent from our Father. Created beings cannot make themselves independent. The only option for created beings is to choose where or upon whom they will be dependent.

Humanity's original choice to depend upon creation is what made us independent from our Creator. Today, each soul is born into the heritage of the first man's choice. However, God came as a man to become the Man to return the choice of dependence to every man. Now, each man partnered with the Man may begin aggressively pushing everyone toward making their own choice of spiritual dependence by imparting a touch that mercilessly forces every soul in his presence to live a life of material independence.

Part 2
A Co-Defining Authority

As a man begins asserting himself as a self-defining authority, he'll quickly realize that he is the single greatest threat to everyone around him in becoming a unique authority. As a result, before a man irreparably incites the wrath of the Creator, creation, and every human creator, he'll do well to select a woman to form a co-creational partnership in the likeness of the first partnership. Consequently, a woman's body is designed and, therefore, delights in portraying feminine creation, thus allowing her to assist her masculine partner in becoming a material authority who does not violate her spiritual authority. Since a woman's soul holds the same position of spiritual authority as a man's, she may choose to consciously submit her body to her husband so she might assist him in growing into a masculine creator capable of protecting the sovereignty of everyone without infringing upon the sovereignty of anyone.

Section 4
Spiritual Authorities

Marriage brings together two unique, world-making authorities, who each exist within their own separate, intimate, and eternal union with the Masculine Creator. The marital partnership between a man and a woman is what allows two souls to unite and work together toward creating the same unique world. Similar to how God touches both souls to make two spiritual world makers, both souls must touch their two minds, two hearts, and two bodies to make the two inner world makers required to bring forth the same material world. Amidst marriage, two spiritual authorities co-create together by designing their union to mirror the first union, where the original Masculine Creator and the feminine creation united to bring forth their world of unique worlds for their race of unique world makers.

Chapter 10
Two Sovereigns, One Sphere

The world came into existence through the union of the Masculine Creator and the feminine creation. Children are often taught that the universe came into being as if it were a magical event where God did everything in isolation. However, while making His world, the Creator used words to express what He desired, almost as if He was communicating with someone. The point of such a realization is not to conclude that creation existed before the beginning. Instead, the point is to realize that the Creator brought forth creation from the material void to be His partner. Similarly, God desires to touch, shape, and breathe into the spiritual void within each soul to make a unique world maker who will then know how to go forth to touch His material world in a way that will bring forth their own unique world.

When God first spoke to the material void—as if it were someone—our mother awakened in response to her Creator's expectation. Creation, having never known anyone other than the One, remained submissively silent to obediently fulfill the desires of her Beloved. She wanted God to shape her into the object of His desire, and what God desired was a world that would affectionately cultivate His world makers.

The difference in intimacy between how God led creation during the first five days and on the sixth day is telling. During the first five days, God spoke to creation. However, on the sixth day, God touched, shaped, and breathed a creator into creation. The partnership between God and creation, although profound, is still a full magnitude less intimate than the partnership between God and humanity.

Since God is infinite and spiritual, His union with the finite material realm will always remain limited. However, God's love for creation impelled Him to bridge this limitation with humanity. As we are both spiritual and material, each human being is the conduit designed to conduct the Creator's love out toward creation and creation's love back toward her Creator. We are the children who arose amidst the original union between our spiritual Father and our material mother. As a race of unique world makers, humanity is the culmination and continuation of the first partnership. Therefore, we each exist to become a unique world maker through God's touch so that we might touch His world to make our own unique world, thereby fulfilling our Father's desire for a race of unique world makers and our mother's desire for a world of unique worlds.

Maintaining a submissive dependence upon the Creator and an authoritative independence from creation is the ideal position from which a race of unique world makers might make a world of unique worlds. However, God made two human beings, not one. Therefore, the ideal world-making partnership is for one to uniquely portray the authoritatively independent Creator and the second to uniquely portray the submissively dependent creation.

Marriage is the sublime encapsulation of God's intended design to unite His spiritual realm with creation's material realm through each human being's inner realm. First, within marriage, neither soul touches the other. Each spiritual void must be touched, shaped, and breathed into by only the One. The concept of soul-mates, although quaint, is an abhorrent perversion in God's eyes. No spiritual soul mates with anything or anyone other than the One. Only the Soulmate may touch, shape, and breathe into each soul's void of infinite emptiness to bring forth one bearing a never-before-seen likeness of His uniqueness.

A marriage begins when two independent, authoritative, and unique world makers—who each live amidst their own spiritual partnership with God—decide to form an inner partnership. Amidst marriage, two souls meld their two inner realms into one. As inviolate spiritual authorities, both sovereigns may then touch, shape, and breathe their world-making knowledge, desires, and intentions into both minds, hearts, and bodies, while God alone is touching both souls. Marriage is the ideal co-creational union because the Creator will have a masculine conduit to conduct His love toward creation, and creation will have a feminine conduit to conduct her love back toward her Creator. Although each married couple will create their own unique world through their own unique union, if a couple offers their partnership to the first partnership, then they'll find themselves participating in a world-making union far larger than just their world-making union.

Marriage is an inner partnership, not a spiritual one or a material one. The Creator's spiritual union with each soul is exclusive, while creation's material union with a couple's world is all-inclusive. Therefore, a couple's union is only private within their shared inner realm, where they alone may touch one another's minds, hearts, and bodies to shape one another's thoughts, emotions, and actions.

Amidst the material realm, creation expects a couple's world to follow her lead toward greater interconnection within her as God's world of unique worlds. As a result, our mother will ceaselessly bring anatomical treasures and other world makers to the couple's bodies for partnership. Either spouse attempting to gain exclusive authority over either material body or their world will arouse our mother's wrath, just as attempting to gain exclusive authority over either spiritual soul will arouse our Father's wrath. Only the couple's united inner realm will remain exclusively under their authority.

After God created the first man and woman, He declared that their union would result in one flesh. Whenever the Creator specifically identifies something by name, we should pay close attention. God called the marital union one flesh because He intended a human couple to bind their two minds, two hearts, and two bodies into one united inner realm. However, a couple's one inner flesh will not make the couple think, feel, and act like the same person. Instead, becoming a united conduit between the Creator's spiritual realm and creation's material realm requires one to uniquely think, feel, and act like the Masculine Creator and the second to uniquely think, feel, and act like the feminine creation.

A man's masculinity is most distinct when it is clear he is not the woman standing next to him. Likewise, a woman's femininity is most distinct when it is clear she is not the man standing next to her. For this reason, both souls must have a hand in how both minds think, both hearts feel, and both bodies act. Beneficially opposed, co-created contrast enhances the splendor of both spouses as the couple lives out their own unique representation of the first partnership.

The supreme example of how a partnership functions in beneficial opposition to one another is the first partnership. As the Creator and creation progressed through the first seven days, creation modeled femininity by submitting unconditionally to her masculine partner. A married woman may do likewise, but only if her soul is actively shaping the thoughts, emotions, and actions of her masculine spouse. The authoritative thoughts, emotions, and actions arising from a male body must be co-created by both souls. Likewise, the submissive thoughts, emotions, and actions rising from a female body must also be co-created by both souls. The making of two beneficially opposed characters for a couple's one world-making effort requires each to exert equal authority within the same united inner realm of one flesh.

When God referenced the first man's desire for a woman, He proclaimed that a man would leave his father and mother to be united with his wife. However, for the first man, no biological parents existed for him to leave. God's original declaration may have been referencing the eventuality of biological parents that each successive generation of men would leave before selecting a spouse for world-making. However, God's initial declaration was actually referencing how the first man, and each successive man, must leave the world created by the Father and the mother so that—as a masculine creator—he might go forth to unite with a woman to conceive a distinctly unique world from within God's world.

Our spiritual Father rules, fills, and subdues the spiritual realm, while our material mother rules, fills, and subdues the material realm. However, each human being rules, fills, and subdues their inner realm. Humanity's inner realm connects the spiritual realm to the material realm, making mankind the epicenter of all orchestration. God is the source, we are the epicenter, and creation is the world of unique worlds that everyone desires. The man who leaves the world created by our spiritual Father and material mother may then unite with a woman to co-create one new epicenter of world-making authority that will interconnect all three realms into one new, triune world amidst the Trinity's world.

Amidst marriage, both souls are sovereign, world-making beings. However, since a couple cannot unite their two souls, they instead unite their two spheres of sovereignty. Once merged, both sovereigns will hold equal spiritual authority over both minds, hearts, and bodies, as well as all their material possessions. However, the two souls who've agreed to unite their sovereign spheres will remain separate sovereign authorities. Consensually binding two world makers together within the same sovereign sphere is the only way that two may begin co-creating as one.

A world-making man and a world-making woman join together in matrimony to fulfill the world-making intentions of two as if they were one. Each man and each woman desires to make their own unique world with its own visionary existence, meaningful identity, and principal purpose. Marriage amplifies the capabilities of two world makers by allowing each to mentally perceive, emotionally feel, and physically fulfill the principal purpose of both as they make the same unique world.

The basis for a couple's union within their inner realm is their individual union with God in the spiritual realm. Each soul begins their union with God as His spiritual void, similar to how creation began her union with God as His material void. Both spouses must individually submit to the Soulmate so each might be touched, shaped, and breathed into their own likeness of His uniqueness. Then, amidst each soul's timeless, spaceless, and matterless spiritual union with the eternal Partner, it is only natural for each to begin searching for a marital partner so they might attain the most efficient and most effective means for expressing their spiritual union with God through an inner union with another.

God is each soul's Masculine Creator. Each soul is God's feminine creation. Submitting to God as His bride provides each soul with unique knowledge regarding how they, as a feminine creation, unite with the Masculine Creator to bring forth uniqueness. Marriage provides two souls with the ideal position from which to robustly express the totality of each partner's spiritual union with the Soulmate. As two souls craft their two minds, hearts, and bodies toward expressing the two beings they've experienced in the spiritual realm, they'll find they have all they need to express their spiritual partnership with God through their marital partnership with one another.

As a void of infinite emptiness, each soul exerts an immeasurable feminine pull upon Infinite Fullness. Nothing is more arousing to God than a submissive soul of infinite emptiness. Our Masculine Creator desires to push into our soul's embryonic void to conceive one who is unlike anyone. Such a wondrous, faith-based experience of timeless spiritual manifestation is what gives human marriage its visionary, meaningful purpose. Anyone who is becoming a unique one—through their own spiritual union with the One—must create the inner and material means to express those spiritual experiences.

Once two unique ones are bound amidst their own marital partnership of inner oneness, a man will offer his masculine mind, heart, and body to his wife so she might enrich his material portrayal of masculinity with her spiritual experiences. At the same time, a woman will likewise offer her feminine mind, heart, and body to her husband so he might enrich her material portrayal of femininity with his spiritual experiences. As equally authoritative world makers, a couple co-creates together to craft one masculine creator and one feminine creation who will uniquely think, feel, and act out what both souls are spiritually experiencing with the Soulmate. The man who is developing into a masculine creator amidst his spiritual union with God and his inner union with his wife will steadily develop from one who is able to only uphold his authority as a world maker into one who is able to simultaneously uphold the authority of two world makers who are making one unique world, in preparation for him doing likewise with every world maker who is making God's world into one world of unique worlds.

Chapter 11
Obstructing Two Takers

God originally designed the union between a man and a woman to enable humanity's world-making efforts. Unfortunately, fallen humanity's present world-taking efforts have irreparably damaged marriage. Today, when two lightless, loveless, and lifeless souls unite within one shared inner realm, their intent is not to make with one another but to take from one another. Even souls who've returned to the Soulmate will continue unconsciously employing taking-tactics for the remainder of their days. Therefore, if a man intends to hold the line against any taker, he must begin holding the line against his soul and his wife's soul as two takers bound together within the same inner realm.

Both men and women are takers. Since we all begin as untouched souls, everyone is desperate to materially take from others what we hope will spiritually make us like God. As fallen beings, both men and women enter matrimony teeming with conscious and unconscious taking-tactics. Although everyone has their own personalized strategies and levels of ambition, we all seek to be the one who rules, fills, and subdues all, for the good of all, of course. Therefore, a masculine creator will take it upon himself to draw the lines that obstruct and expose the taking-tactics of both spouses in a way that leads the couple away from taking and toward world-making.

A man's ability to obstruct world takers and lead them toward being world makers begins by obstructing the most dangerous, devious, and depraved taker of all—himself. Furthermore, marriage provides a man with the supreme arena to expose and obstruct himself as a lightless, loveless, and lifeless soul. After all, nothing is more tempting to a man desperate to look, feel, and act like the Masculine Creator than sexually dominating one who robustly embodies the entire universal whole of feminine creation.

Many efforts have been made to expose the root of each man's sexual exploitation of women. The problem with all such efforts is that they attempt to pin the problem on the way a man is sexually thinking, feeling, and acting. If a man's sexual issues arose from improper thoughts, emotions, and actions, then merely changing the way he thinks, feels, and acts would eliminate all the issues. However, as all parties involved eventually discover, a man's problem lies beneath his mind, heart, and body. Just as the first man's soul attempted to consume a piece of feminine creation to make himself like God, so every present-day man is sexually consuming the material body of his feminine partner to make himself look, feel, and act more like the Masculine Creator.

When a fallen man marries a woman, his foremost desire is to sexually exploit the feminine mind, heart, and body of his spouse. Sex holds such boundless appeal for a man because a woman's body bears the likeness of the entire material universe. For example, a woman's curves are so captivating to a man because they each suggest there is a world being held elegantly within her, just like God's world of unique worlds. For a fallen man, sexually dominating a feminine woman is akin to materially dominating the entire feminine universe. Therefore, sex with a woman is seen as the foremost material means for a fallen man to attain his spiritual ascension into Perfection.

Only the Masculine Creator rules, fills, and subdues the whole of feminine creation. A fallen man hopes that sexually dominating a woman—who robustly embodies God's world of unique worlds—will somehow make him like God. Unfortunately, as every man eventually discovers, sexual intercourse exists to make material world makers, not spiritual world makers. A spiritual world maker is conceived, born, and grown only as the Masculine Creator dominates and inseminates a submissive soul. Then, a couple's sexual intercourse becomes the means by which both may express together what each has already experienced with the Soulmate. Additionally, sexual intercourse also holds the possibility of allowing a couple to participate with the Creator and creation in the making of material world makers.

The more intimately, repetitiously, and intensely a lifeless soul of infinite emptiness touches a material object, the more rapidly the atoms comprising that object will crumble into darkness, decay, and death. Consequently, a woman's beauty often fades rapidly after engaging extensively in sexual intimacy because her partner's soul is spiritually feasting upon the vitality, effervescence, and holistic splendor of her feminine form. However, abstaining from sexual intercourse to protect the beauty, longevity, and life of a woman's body is not a viable solution. The woman who denies all men sexual access will only succeed in delaying decay. Any man in her proximity who looks upon her will still exert the same result, albeit with a decreased effect. Furthermore, the ultimate problem is her own untouched soul of infinite emptiness, which is bound inside her body and draining the light, love, and life from her femininity.

Material creation lives to express the spiritual Creator and His spiritually unique ones. Any atoms within the immediate proximity of a soul will unite with that soul to express them under the assumption that they are being touched by the One who is Light, Love, and Life. As a fallen soul intimately, repetitiously, and intensely touches the atoms of creation, those atoms will submissively unite to and obediently express the likeness of their spiritual being. As a result, abstaining from intimacy with feminine creation or a feminine woman cannot save a man from seeing, feeling, and experiencing his vacuous, spiritual nature. Every material atom near a man's soul will submissively unite with and express him as a void of infinite emptiness. Sadly, all forms of femininity wither into darkness, decay, and death amidst the inexpressible despair of being materially united to one devoid of spiritual Light, Love, and Life.

The man who commits to obstructing himself as a taker must face the tragic truth that every touch he places upon feminine creation—and his feminine spouse—will bring forth expressions of his lightless, loveless, and lifeless soul. Furthermore, a masculine creator must humbly request feminine creation and his feminine spouse to knowingly sacrifice themselves in assisting him to see, feel, and experience his lifelessness so that, with each fresh revelation, he might turn with even greater spiritual desperation toward the Creator. However, creation and a woman will only agree to such a request as long as a man acknowledges everything they bring forth from his touch as good. Our orchestrational mother—and the women who bear her likeness—understand the sacrifice required of them amidst the present fallen age. However, they'll withdraw from a man's touch the moment he judges anything they bring forth to express him as anything other than a good and pleasing approximation of his spiritual nature.

Although a man will never succeed in fully expunging the taker's likeness from his soul, each moment of exposure with his spouse and creation is an opportunity to return afresh to a deeper union with the Soulmate. As creation and a woman sense how deeply their sacrificial service is helping a man to become a more effective masculine creator, they'll draw upon their feminine reserves to entice him into even deeper levels of intimacy. Then, a man will discover how every expression resulting from his touch leads to the same end. If creation and a woman swoon beneath him, a man will sense his infinite desire to consume the glory of their expressions, obligating his soul to instantaneously turn toward the Infinite One. Conversely, if creation and a woman bring forth expressions from a man's touch that lie on the opposite end of the spectrum, then he'll also be obligated to instantaneously turn toward God.

While a man's taking-tactics are rather obvious—as personified by his fixation on sexually dominating an embodiment of feminine creation so he might look, feel, and act like the Masculine Creator—a woman's taking-tactics are far more varied and subtle. A man desires to be the One who rules, fills, and subdues all. Conversely, a woman desires to be the one beside the One who rules, fills, and subdues all so that—when she's ready—she can remove Him, take His world, and then be the One who rules, fills, and subdues all.

While each man harbors deep-seated rage that no one recognizes him as the Successful One, a woman harbors deep-seated rage that the One did not recognize her as His Desirable One. A woman is born knowing that her soul is untouched, unloved, and undesired. As deeply as each man knows he has failed to be the One, a woman knows she has failed to attract the One. It is this innate knowledge of her undesirability before the Masculine Creator that festers within a woman's soul and impels her to use every material atom within her reach to enact justice upon the Suitor who first spurned her. What a fallen woman does not understand is that God does not desire a partner like Himself. As Infinite Fullness, the Masculine Creator is only attracted to a spouse of infinite emptiness, which is the one thing every fallen woman is trying not to be.

Since God has rejected every soul attempting to be like Him as undesirable, each woman feels that she is responsible to elevate herself into a desirable partner for the Masculine Creator. While men fixate largely on sex for their exaltation into Perfection, women have far more varied strategies to achieve equality with God. For example, some women dream about a grand marital ceremony where an entire gathering, event, and day is centered upon them. They innately perceive such a spectacle as a beacon that would pierce the heavens, awaken the Creator to His mistake, and impel Him to swoop down to steal her away from the Earth. Still, other women have a strong inclination toward bearing children. After all, conceiving world makers is certainly the way to gain the World Maker's favor. Even more women aspire to arouse the Masculine Creator's jealousy by uniting with as many masculine creators as possible to display their supreme desirability before the ever-watchful gaze of the One.

What a man must understand is that all the taking-tactics his feminine counterpart is employing against him are merely being honed and refined in preparation for their ultimate employment against God. After all, a woman's soul is not interested in merely being a feminine creation, she wants to be the feminine creation. Each woman wants to be God's world, not a man's world. Therefore, no man will ever measure up to a woman's standard of masculinity because she is only interested in capturing, dethroning, and decapitating the One.

Once any woman feels she's captured a male through her preferred tactic of promiscuity, matrimony, or being a mommy, she will immediately start looking for a greater man to ensnare. Even if a couple stays together, the process continues as each woman prepares herself to capture, dethrone, and decapitate the Man. Amidst a marriage that lasts decades, this process is depicted by how a woman slowly exiles her spouse to select rooms, then to the garage, and finally to a cave in the backyard. The embittered, untouched soul within a woman is using her feminine mind, heart, and body to attract a man so she might take his world, position, and identity until she alone rules, fills, and subdues all. Still, all a woman's efforts are merely preparing her for the supreme aim of attracting God so she might take His world, position, and identity.

A woman's taking-tactics will always begin by intentionally placing herself in a position of inferiority. Then, as she pulls her partner toward herself, a woman will perceive that she is elevating herself in relation to her previously superior partner. However, like all fallen beings, a woman is not interested in equality; she wants superiority. Therefore, the moment a woman has achieved parity with her present masculine partner, she'll immediately lose interest and start looking for a greater representation of the One to continue her ascension to Perfection. Once a woman finally feels she is ready to attract, capture, and dethrone God, she'll look around at human masculinity and scoff at how there is no longer any man superior to her, leaving only the One.

Nowhere is the ultimate end of a woman's taking-tactics more evident than during an ugly divorce where she's taking as much of a man's world, position, and identity as possible. The more thoroughly a woman captures, dethrones, and decapitates a human man, the more confident she'll be in her ultimate effort to do likewise to the Man. The bitterness festering within every woman's lightless, loveless, and lifeless soul impels her to make an example out of anyone who bears the likeness of the Suitor who first spurned her. Although each woman seeks to exalt herself over God, exile Him from His world, and remove Him permanently as the Creator, such an effort is simply materially portraying what every fallen being desires to spiritually do to God.

The man who obstructs himself from taking is ready to do likewise for his wife. Then, the man courageous enough to obstruct his wife's taking-tactics is the one who may do the same for anyone. In fact, a woman who lives spiritually alongside God will feel an obligation to increase, and not decrease, the complexity of her taking-tactics. After all, the best way for a wife to help her husband to become a masculine one obstructing anyone attempting to be the One is to simultaneously be his greatest challenge and his greatest ally.

Obstructing two world takers intertwined within one inner flesh, is not a winning proposition. However, a man who is already facing and embracing the unalterable truth is not interested in winning. Fallen men enter into marriage to sexually dominate an embodiment of feminine creation so they'll win by looking, feeling, and acting like the Masculine Creator. Likewise, fallen women enter into marriage so they'll win by being the one who captures, dethrones, and decapitates one who is like the Masculine One. Therefore, the man who is synchronously and simultaneously obstructing his soul and his wife's soul from taking from one another is a masculine creator who will live the rest of his days obstructing anyone attempting to be the One.

Chapter 12
Making Two Makers

Human beings were never designed to use material creation to make themselves into spiritual creators. We were designed to be made into spiritual creators by God so we might authoritatively lead material creation toward making our own unique world, so our mother might continue growing into God's world of unique worlds. As created creators, we may only make material expressions of who we already are from the inside out. Therefore, a couple's first task—after being spiritually made by the World Maker—is to inwardly make two mentally illuminated, emotionally flowing, and physically moving world makers.

Without first being made by Light, Love, and Life into a unique spiritual being of light, love, and life, we cannot make our own material expressions of light, love, and life. Fallen beings materially take from the outside in because they've never been spiritually made from the inside out. Conversely, a sovereign world maker makes from the inside out, based upon how the World Maker has already spiritually made them, from the inside out. Therefore, a man offers his soul to God to be made into a unique, spiritual world maker so he might do likewise as he inwardly leads his wife in the making of two inner world makers. Then, amidst the couple's growing skill in making inner world makers, from the inside out, they'll begin leading all humanity toward making a race of unique world makers who will work together toward making Mother Nature into our world of unique worlds from the inside out.

Unlike God, who's always existed as the World Maker, we each must first be made into a spiritual world maker before attempting to make our own material world. However, even after our soul has been touched, shaped, and breathed into by the World Maker, we're each still not quite ready to create our own unique world. Instead, each sovereign soul must enter their inner realm to make a mental, emotional, and physical likeness of the spiritual world maker God has already made. Only after we've been spiritually made into unique world makers by God may we craft our own inner representation of the likeness of Uniqueness that we, and we alone, bear so we might enter God's world as spiritual world makers, and as inner world makers ready to make our own material worlds.

In marriage, two sovereign souls unite their two inner realms so they might co-create together as one. Then, as one co-creative union, a couple may open their two minds, hearts, and bodies to one another so that, together, they might co-create one inner masculine world maker and one inner feminine world maker that express the two unique ones that God has already made. Just as God made a likeness for His spiritual self before entering material creation, each spiritual sovereign must make an inner likeness for themselves—aligned with the spiritual likeness that God has already made—so they, too, might enter the material realm and make their own unique world.

God makes a spiritual likeness for us in His spiritual realm. Then, creation makes a material likeness for us in her material realm. However, it is our job to connect the two by making a mental, emotional, and physical likeness—our inner likeness—that will connect the spiritual likeness crafted for us by God and the material likeness crafted for us by creation. Each human being is the triune connection designed to uniquely interconnect all three realms into one.

The inner realm is where a spiritual sovereign—or two married spiritual sovereigns—practice the highest form of orchestration, making world makers. An unmarried individual may only make one inner world maker. However, a married couple consensually bound together within the same inner realm may create two beneficially opposed inner world makers, one masculine and one feminine, to ensure their partnership effectively aligns with the first partnership.

As two inviolate spiritual authorities, a couple inwardly co-creates one masculine world maker and one feminine world maker that will work together toward the same end. If a couple does not engage in their inner realm as creative equals, then they'll go to war over who rules, fills, and subdues both minds, hearts, and bodies. Engaging in war inside one shared inner realm always results in traumatic damage to both partners' minds, hearts, and bodies. Sometimes, those wounds will heal over time. Other times they will not. The best approach is to avoid war in the inner realm just as diligently as we avoid war in the material realm.

The forceful nature of masculine push and feminine pull will prove extremely useful within one shared inner realm. As the repulsive partner, a man will delight in pushing both souls toward the Masculine Creator to continually glean more of the spiritual experiences he needs to inspire his material portrayal of masculinity. At the same time, as the attractive partner, a woman will delight in arousing both souls to pull vigorously upon the Masculine Creator to continually glean more of the spiritual experiences she needs to inspire her material portrayal of femininity.

The male and female bodies were designed to follow only their soul's spiritual authority, not God's. Authority flows from God into each soul. Then, from each soul into their inner realm. And finally, out through each soul's inner realm into creation. If a couple's souls do not provide their minds, hearts, and bodies with their own authoritative spiritual leadership, then their inner realm will have no access to God's authority, compelling both minds, hearts, and bodies to look outward for leadership. However, external authorities cannot lead a couple's minds, hearts, and bodies toward thinking, feeling, and acting uniquely. Consequently, if a couple desires their own unique marital union and their own unique world, then they must ensure that their two minds, hearts, and bodies are looking only to their souls for leadership, while each soul looks only to God.

When making two world makers from within one shared inner realm, the spiritual authority of both souls must remain inviolate. If either soul is secretly strategizing to gain dominance over the other, then that intention will corrupt the thoughts, emotions, and actions of both. The male and female bodies are not created equal. One is designed to uniquely express the spiritual Creator, and the other to uniquely express material creation. However, both bodies need to know that the two sovereigns directing their thoughts, emotions, and actions each remain equal world-making authorities. If either body senses their soul is being slighted, then they'll immediately start withdrawing from the inner partnership.

Co-creation requires two equal spiritual authorities because each partner's body will always remain loyal to its own soul. If either mind, heart, or body senses their original spiritual authority is being undermined, then they'll turn defensive and/or aggressive. Maintaining spiritual equality while co-creating the masculine and the feminine inner likeness that the couple needs to express their two spiritual likenesses of Uniqueness is essential for the marriage intent on creating the two inner world makers needed to bring forth the same material world.

A female body wants to fully commit to the submissive role of feminine creation. Anything less than utter material submission, worship, and adoration of her masculine partner will degrade her portrayal of how creation submits to, worships, and adores the Creator. At the same time, a woman's soul will remain hyper-sensitive to how vulnerable this makes her body. Additionally, a woman's intuitive sense of the fallen impulse within her spouse will further infuse her with justifiable fear. As a result, the moment a woman's soul senses her body is being used, misused, or abused, she'll halt her material portrayal of feminine submission until she can reassert her spiritual authority. Unfortunately, such a shift is heartbreaking for the female body, which delights in uniquely portraying creation's submissive love toward the Masculine Creator.

The female body desires to be delighted in as she portrays how her soul and creation unite with the Creator. Similarly, the male body does not wish to be degraded in his portrayal of the Masculine One. Therefore, the dignity of the male body and the delight of the female body require both souls to remain equal spiritual authorities so that each partner's body might remain submerged in their respective role as they, together, uniquely portray the first partnership.

A man and a woman both become world makers by individually submitting their souls to God. Then, as equal spiritual authorities, both beings may touch their two minds, two hearts, and two bodies so that, together, they might make the masculine world maker and the feminine world maker they need to make the same unique world. Then, as each soul invests the inner likeness that corresponds to their body's material likeness, the couple may stroll forth together into creation's material realm as one unique masculine creator and one unique feminine creation who will unite and co-create together to bring forth the same unique world. Consequently, the man who is refining the art of making unique world makers alongside an equal spiritual authority within one shared inner realm is being made ready to make unique world makers alongside billions of equal spiritual authorities within one shared material realm.

Section 5
Inner Creators

The couple who unites amidst one shared inner realm will create the masculine world maker and the feminine world maker they need to bring forth their unique world. First, both souls must lead both minds toward forming a masculine and a feminine image. Next, both souls must lead both hearts toward generating a masculine aura and a feminine aura. Lastly, both souls must lead both bodies toward developing a masculine style of action and a feminine style of action so that, as two, a couple might think, feel, and act as one toward orchestrating the same unique world.

Chapter 13
Seeing Two Unique Ones

The central illuminated image within one's mind is always a cognitive depiction of our spiritual being. Once two unite within the same inner realm, their central illuminated image will consist of one masculine likeness and one feminine likeness so that the couple might exude their ruling authority together. Additionally, the luminous depiction that each mind forms to express its spiritual sovereign will slowly shape the way their heart feels and their body acts, particularly if that image is held over years and decades. Once two sovereigns unite within one shared inner realm, their two minds will labor to make the light-based likeness of the two world makers they require for making the same unique world.

A couple must first spiritually be the two unique ones they desire their minds to see. Once each spouse's mind is gazing into both souls to perceive the two spiritual world makers that God has already made, a man's mind will begin forming an illuminated central image of unstoppable masculinity while a woman's mind will begin forming an illuminated central image of irresistible femininity. In marriage, both sovereigns must inspire both minds in the craftsmanship of both illuminated images. Then, as each sovereign adorns the mental image that corresponds to their body, both world makers may wield a shared ruling authority of light over their united inner realm and their personal portion of creation's material realm.

Our central illuminated image is what translates the timeless, spaceless, and matterless spiritual being within one's soul into a cognitive form that will inwardly display the unique one that the Maker has already made. After creating our central illuminated image, our spiritual being may then step into and adorn our mental likeness to begin walking through our inner realm as the gardener who is authoritatively ruling over, and caring for each of our growing emotions and ripening actions. Consequently, if our heart and body cannot first mentally see a cognitive representation of our unique spiritual being, then our inner realm will remain unable to emotionally feel and physically express our spiritual likeness of Uniqueness.

The mental image a mind forms to represent the unique one within their soul will never be a perfect replication. Instead, each mind will form its own mental approximation of the spiritual being they see as their sovereign authority. After all, a timeless, spaceless, and matterless spiritual being will always lose much as Mother Nature's anatomical splendor begins shaping a cognitive likeness for them that will effectively correlate to her finite material realm of time, space, and matter. Fortunately, everyone's inner realm is custom designed by the Creator and affectionately cultivated by creation to assist each in translating their spiritual likeness of Uniqueness into something that will effectively translate out through their material body and into the natural world.

Nowhere in all creation are the rules of time, space, and matter more flexible than in the human mind. Within our minds, we may imagine things we've never seen, go places we've never been, and be someone we could never be. The mind is the first place a resurrected sovereign begins expressing their spiritual likeness of Uniqueness. As the ruling instrument of the inner realm, every mind is designed to form its own central illuminated image so its spiritual sovereign might be inwardly seen as an independent, authoritative, and unique world maker.

Our mind's central illuminated image aligns our spiritual likeness to our material likeness. Therefore, the masculine or feminine image within our mind must hold to the basic structures of our human form. As a result, each spouse's mental likeness should have a human head, abdomen, and limbs. Any attempt to force the mind to create a central illuminated image that diverges too far from the human form will make it incompatible, irrelevant, and ineffective at connecting our spiritual likeness to our material likeness.

A central illuminated image is a cognitive prism designed to project a timeless, spaceless, and matterless spiritual being through the limited constraints of the human body. The temptation to create a mental image unlike anything is rooted in the fallen impulse to destroy all God has made and remake all things into a new, better, and perfect likeness. Therefore, a submissive soul displays their reverence for God, respect for creation, and recognition of every human creator by restricting their inner mental likeness to the bounds of their material human likeness.

Being born with an untouched soul—who is nothing, nowhere, and no one—has crippled the creative capacity of every human mind. Our mind is designed to gaze into our soul and form a mental approximation of the spiritually unique one that God has already conceived from within our void. However, since everyone's mind is born staring into an untouched soul of infinite emptiness, each human mind has grown bored and turned away from the spiritual realm and toward the material realm. Should a soul return to God so that He might touch, shape, and breathe a unique sovereign being of world-making authority into existence, the newly risen one will then discover that their mind is no longer looking in their direction. As a result, the first inner task of a unique one—or two in the case of marriage—is to authoritatively arrest the attention of their mind.

The mental image formed by a mind looking out into the material realm for inspiration will always end up as a Frankenstein-like monstrosity pieced together from countless external representations of masculinity or femininity. As a result, each mind's central illuminated image will remain completely incompatible with the independent,

101

authoritative, and unique spiritual sovereign God desires to conceive from within their submissive soul. Attempting to project one's spiritual likeness of Uniqueness through a mental prism crafted in the likeness of another man or woman will utterly inhibit every effort a couple makes toward making their own unique world within God's world.

The man who mentally depicts another man as his central illuminated image will feel worthlessness and intentionally act in a way that leads toward failure amidst his innate disgust at being just another masculine replication. Likewise, the woman who mentally depicts another woman as her central illuminated image will feel undesirable and intentionally act in a way that leads toward rejection amidst her innate despair at being just another feminine replication. The solution to such counterproductive thoughts, emotions, and actions begins by forcibly reorienting one's mind away from the material realm and back toward the spiritual realm. Only when a mind sees a unique one—brought forth by the Unique One—will it discard all previous attempts to depict masculinity or femininity and finally begin forming a central illuminated image of uniqueness.

A living spiritual being touches their mind first because it is the closest to the spiritual realm and the least restrained by the material realm. Once two living spiritual beings unite within the same inner realm, their two minds will find they have the two spiritual sovereigns needed to make one central illuminated image of two unique ones. Then, both minds will begin designing an image to represent their spiritual sovereign before bringing both side-by-side as one united, central illuminated image composed of a uniquely masculine one and a uniquely feminine one.

A man's mental likeness of unstoppable masculinity must cognitively represent how both souls experience the Masculine Creator. At the same time, a woman's mental likeness of irresistible femininity must cognitively represent how both souls live as a feminine creation to the Masculine Creator. A man will be primarily focused on how God treats both souls to enrich his portrayal of masculinity, while his spouse will remain primarily focused on how both souls respond to God to enrich her portrayal of femininity. Co-creating partners treasure their spouse's perspective so that they might ensure their material portrayal of masculinity or femininity remains as robust as possible.

No soul has a sex. Only human bodies have a sex. However, each soul is responsible for translating their spiritual experiences—with the Masculine Creator as His feminine creation—into something that may be expressed through both bodies. Marriage is the ideal location to fulfill this task. Having two souls with the two bodies needed to express the totality of what each partner is experiencing with God, and exerting upon God, allows for a robust portrayal of each soul's eternal partnership with the Creator through a couple's marital partnership with one another.

Similar to how our physical body always stands at the epicenter of our mobile portion of the material realm, our central illuminated image always stands at the epicenter of our inner realm. All actions flow from all emotions, and all emotions flow from all thoughts. However, all thoughts flow from the thinker of those thoughts. The way we mentally depict ourselves as the thinker is what makes us the inner source for all our thoughts, emotions, and actions.

An independent, authoritative, and unique spiritual sovereign is the one and only source for a unique world. However, each spiritual sovereign is still responsible for making a mental representation of themselves as the source for their world. Authoritatively directing the mental craftsmanship of a central illuminated image is the first step to a sovereign's rule over their inner realm. Moreover, our central illuminated image is not only a representation of our spiritual authority but the first anatomical adornment that we must enter as a spiritual being to gain access to our inner realm and, eventually, creation's material realm.

When a human mind is touched by a living spiritual being, it will immediately begin crafting luminescent lines to sketch out the perplexing complexity that we are as a spiritual mystery. A human mind—as an integral aspect of creation—responds to the touch of a spiritual authority, similar to the way creation originally responded to the touch of the Authority. Since our first touch as a spiritual being falls upon our mind, it is symbolically characterized by the first material expression God formed on day one, which is why the mind is the domain of illumination.

Once we touch our inner realm as a unique spiritual sovereign, our mind will immediately begin forming the illuminated lines needed to outline the living being God has already brought forth in the spiritual realm. Our soul's void, even beneath the Creator's touch, will always remain within our soul to envelop our unique spiritual being with the medium God prefers for making each one even more unlike anyone. Then, as the Infinite One's touch remains upon us, the infinite void encasing us will be utilized to expand our ever-increasing independence, authority, and uniqueness. At the same time, the moment a growing spiritual being moves away from God's touch, they'll instantly collapse back into the void from which they came. Then, our mind—which up until that moment had been mentally sketching out our splendor—will lose sight of our uniqueness, causing the glowing lines of our central illuminated image to dissipate.

Creation's forms of material light are all saturated with innate information about her Unique One. Likewise, our mind's mental lines of illumination are all saturated with innate information about our uniqueness. Once our spiritual being steps into our central illuminated image, we'll radiate nourishing knowledge throughout our inner realm to saturate our mind, heart, and body with innate information about who we are. When a second spiritual being adorned with a beneficially opposed central illuminated image joins us, the effect upon our inner realm is compounded. Once two hearts and two bodies can mentally see an unstoppable masculine creator and an irresistible feminine creation standing together as equals amidst the same shared inner realm, then flowing emotions and fiery actions will follow.

Despite the excitement inherent in making two central illuminated images, the effort will not take place without difficulties. For example, mentally crafting an image of unstoppable masculinity and irresistible femininity will be resisted by both partners since every man knows he has failed to be like God, and every woman knows she has failed to attract God. The solution is to turn away from trying to be the Masculine Creator and the feminine creation and toward being a unique masculine creator and a unique feminine creation. A man has only failed to be the Masculine Creator. And a woman is only undesirable as the feminine creation. Once a couple turns away from such foolishness, they'll free their united minds, hearts, and bodies to pursue their true desire: to mentally depict, emotionally feel, and physically express one unique masculine creator and one unique feminine creation.

Each time a soul touched by God touches their mind, their central illuminated image will improve. A fallen being drains creation's atoms of light by intimately, repetitiously, and intensely touching her. Inversely, a resurrected being imbues their mind with light by intimately, repetitiously, and intensely touching the atoms within their mind. As a result, the more profoundly, potently, and powerfully a living spiritual sovereign touches their mind, the more striking their central illuminated image will become.

As two spiritual beings touch both minds, their two resulting images will rise together into one central illuminated image. The glowing outline of an unstoppable man and an irresistible woman must be brought close together at the epicenter of one shared inner realm so that, as two, the couple might co-create as one. Although the mental likeness of both sovereigns must retain an unmistakable alignment to both bodies, the nearly limitless creativity of each mind will provide both partners with ample means for differentiation.

Throughout the scriptures, the Creator made a concerted effort to articulate His triune likeness by regularly using blinding light, flowing water, and roiling flames. The reason God so regularly selected these three elemental expressions is that light, water, and fire each correspond to one of His three persons. The Luminous Ruler, the Flowing Filler, and the Fiery Subduer desire every human creator to enrich and expand their inner likeness toward a triune likeness. Therefore, the sovereign who designs their inner likeness aglow with light, flowing with water, and roiling with flames is shaping their likeness toward the One who is Ruling Light, Filling Water, and Subduing Fire.

Resurrected beings—regardless of whether they are married or not—will find their mind exuberant to enrich their central illuminated image of masculinity or femininity with light, water, and fire. As a part of creation's anatomical expanse, every human mind delights in expressing God's triune likeness. Using the elemental expressions born amidst creation to both increase our inner alignment with Uniqueness and enhance our inner likeness of uniqueness pleases our mother.

A unique spiritual sovereign touches their mind to inspire a central illuminated image of who they are as a world maker. Then, as a spiritual being of light—who is created by Light—they'll have a central illuminated image to represent them within their inner realm. In marriage, two spiritual beings inwardly co-create together to bring forth one central illuminated image depicting an unstoppable man alongside an irresistible woman. Then, together, both spiritual sovereigns' may step into their corresponding mental image, so that both hearts might begin to feel, and both bodies might begin to act in alignment with their mental oneness.

Chapter 14
Sparking an Orchestrational Storm

Through the nervous system, which is commonly referred to as the human heart, a world maker fills their inner realm with the potent emotions needed to propel their body to act toward making a unique world within the material realm. Amidst marriage, each sovereign touches both hearts so they might fill their shared sovereign sphere with two independent, interconnected, and interdependent auras of energetic motion. As a result, a couple will conceive the emotionally based, orchestrational storm required to forcefully remake a portion of God's world into their world as they unite their outward pushing, high-pressure aura of masculine emotion to their inward pulling, low-pressure aura of feminine emotion.

After a couple mentally co-creates their two central illuminated images, their next step is to attach an emotional aura to each. Motion is the first and foremost component of feelings. While a mental image is a sketched outline of a unique one, the emotional aura attached to that mental outline is what breathes life into our central illuminated image. Consequently, when a man creates an emotional aura, the direction of his energetic motion should be pushing out from his soul, through his inner realm, and toward creation's material realm. Conversely, when a woman creates her emotional aura, the direction of her energetic motion should be pulling in from creation's material realm, through her inner realm, and toward her soul.

A man's heart wants to generate a high-pressure emotional aura, which is centered on and emanating out from his central illuminated image of unstoppable masculinity. Likewise, a woman's heart wants to generate a low-pressure emotional aura, centered on and emanating inward toward her central illuminated image of irresistible femininity. As the two emotional auras swell from inside the couple's two images, the potent emotions they need to compel the orchestration of their unique world will start filling both bodies and overflowing out into their shared sphere of sovereignty.

The couple who sees themselves as an unstoppable man and an irresistible woman will be mentally profound in their world-making effort. However, the couple who both mentally sees and emotionally feels themselves as an unstoppable man and an irresistible woman will be both mentally profound and emotionally potent in their world-making effort. The closer a couple brings their two central illuminated images—while still retaining a distinction between their two separate sovereign beings—the more their two beneficially opposed emotional auras will spark and spin the orchestrational power they need to make their world from within God's world. After all, everyone knows that a male and a female body spark when brought close together. However, this effect is magnified when a male body emanating an outward pushing emotional aura and a female body emanating an inward pulling emotional aura are brought close together.

An emotional aura is what fills every creator's sovereign sphere with their own outward pushing or inward pulling force. In marriage, a couple is privileged to fill their shared sovereign sphere with both. Making a unique world requires a masculine aura pushing everything and everyone in God's world back to prepare for the orchestration of a unique world. At the same time, making a unique world also requires a feminine aura pulling everything and everyone in God's world closer to prepare the resulting world to become a vital part of God's world. One force without the other will significantly hinder either the independence of the couple's world from God's world or the interconnection of the couple's world with God's world. Both will be needed if a couple desires to create a world that is interdependent with every world and every world maker within God's world of unique worlds.

The human heart uses its energetic motions like sonar. Each emotion is a signal pushed out through the nervous system to bounce off the external environment before being pulled back for deciphering. A couple is in the enviable position of having one heart skilled at pushing emotional signals out toward a predetermined end, while their second heart is skilled at pulling emotional signals back in to decipher their meaning holistically. Then, the emotional results may be reviewed by both spiritual sovereigns in preparation for their next emotional ping. Consequently, the closer a couple brings their two hearts while emotionally pinging creation, the more accurate their outward pushing and inward pulling signals will be.

Since every spiritual being is unique, we're all a mystery to creation. Emotional sonar helps us send subtle communications to Mother Nature before we go blundering about with our actions. Furthermore, our body must fully feel our uniqueness before it can produce confident actions. Therefore, the stronger the two-way emotional sonar emanating from a couple's central illuminated image, the more both bodies will feel like the two unique ones they desire to express out into Mother Nature's ever-changing material expanse.

The human mind is designed to think about the spiritual realm, and the human body is designed to act in the material realm. However, the human heart is designed to interconnect the mind's musings about the spiritual realm with the body's adventures in the material realm. Often, our heart's emotions appear erratic, unfocused, and counterproductive. However, our heart has spent most of its existence conducting emotional signals between a mind staring blankly into a void of infinite emptiness and a body gallivanting haphazardly throughout the void-like material expanse of creation. Without a spiritual being of world-making authority to direct the entire inner realm toward a unique, principal purpose, their heart will remain stuck trying to make meaningful connections between a visionless mind and purposeless body. Understandably, this leads to erratic, unfocused, and counterproductive emotions.

Making a central illuminated image is the first step to restoring orchestrational order to one's inner realm. Once the heart sees the mind's mental depiction of its unique spiritual sovereign, it will begin figuring out how that unique one feels. As a result, an aura of outward pushing or inward pulling emotions will rise from within the central illuminated image to fill the body and sovereign sphere with the potent emotions needed to express the unique one.

Since our emotions forcibly flow forth like water to fill our body and our sovereign sphere, there is little point in trying to control these powerful currents. If we attempt to plug up our emotions, we'll only create a dam that will eventually burst. If we attempt to alter their course, they'll simply find their own way of least resistance out through our body and into creation. The only way to direct our emotional currents is to give our heart what it wants—an illuminated central image displaying a never-before-seen world maker upon which it can attach and generate a never-before-felt aura.

In marriage, two world makers lead their two minds and two hearts toward creating two images with attached auras. As a result, a man will start looking and feeling unstoppable, while a woman starts looking and feeling irresistible. Creating a unique world requires one to be unstoppable in pushing God's world apart and one to be irresistible in pulling a unique world together. Having one partner to simultaneously engender each aura of emotional force is sublimely ideal. Then, the closer the high-pressure aura of an unstoppable man gets to the low-pressure aura of an irresistible woman, the more emotionally potent the couple's orchestrational storm will become.

While motion is central to each heart's emotional currents, a second way to amplify how we feel is to select a color for our aura. In the material realm, a color is created by combining two or more other colors. Similarly, in the inner realm, emotions are created by combining two or more other emotions, and the more exotic the emotional combinations, the more potent the resulting sensations.

Mixing basic but seemingly incompatible emotions, like anger and kindness, will produce a provocatively potent emotional hue. The more emotions a couple mixes into their two auras, the more potent their union will feel. Furthermore, any emotions used in the creation of an aura will be retained in trace elements within that aura. Then, as the situational complexities of the material realm appear, both bodies may draw upon a rich, diverse, and potent emotional reserve to propel their actions.

The World Maker has regularly displayed His triune nature with elemental light, water, and fire. At the same time, we were given our triune likeness of mental illumination, emotional currents, and fiery actions to aid us in making our world in alignment with how the Trinity made the world. As a result, our mind wants to portray us in the luminous likeness of the Ruling Father. Our heart wants to portray us in the flowing likeness of the Filling Spirit. And our body wants to portray us in the fiery likeness of the Subduing Son. Consequently, shaping our inner likeness in harmony with the Creator's triune likeness is a provocative way to display our uniqueness to creation as one who is being touched by and growing into the likeness of, the Triune One.

Should a couple wish to further amplify their triune nature, they may augment their emotional potency by choosing one of the triune elements to characterize the motion and color of their aura. A sovereign with a strong mental affinity will find that feeling the motion and color of their aura as light will make them even more mentally profound. Similarly, a sovereign with a particularly strong emotional affinity will find that feeling the motion and color of their aura as water will make them even more emotionally potent. And a sovereign with a particularly strong physical affinity will find that feeling the motion and color of their aura as fire will make them even more physically powerful. Once a marital partnership of two sovereigns elementally augments their two auras, each will have expressed their inner creative expertise in mental light, emotional water, or physical fire. Then, the final remaining element may be depicted in a co-created color moving about, around, and through their two elementally augmented auras.

A couple's two hearts grow together by creating two emotional auras of beneficially opposed motion, color, and elemental fury. However, like the mind, the heart retains inexhaustible means for customization. The three elements used by the Trinity each exist in the full spectrum of color and temperature in the material realm, making them ideal for customizing each emotional aura. Additionally, augmenting the functional texture of each aura will significantly alter the way it feels and the actions it propels. A subduer's aura may exert a soothing warmth, warding flames, or a combusting fury. A filler's aura may generate an inviting mist, a rushing stream, or a merciless tsunami. And a ruler's aura may project a soft light, an awakening beacon, or a blinding rage. Each aura should be customized to express both sovereigns while enabling both bodies to act in accordance with the couple's combined world-making intentions.

The sovereigns who lead their hearts toward creating two united auras of elemental motion, color, and function will spark their own orchestrational storm. Consequently, mentally seeing and emotionally feeling an unstoppable man and an irresistible woman will engender profound thoughts and potent emotions. An unstoppable man pushes the world-making intentions of both souls through his masculine image and aura straight into his body. At the same time, an irresistible woman helps by using her feminine image and aura to pull the world-making intentions of both souls through her masculine counterpart and into her body to ensure a fertile insemination of material creation. Once two mentally illuminated and emotionally flowing world makers are creating as one, their bodies will be aroused to unite in creation's material realm based upon how the couple is uniting in their inner realm, which is expressing how each soul is uniting with the World Maker in His spiritual realm.

Chapter 15
Turning Different into Unique

There is nothing new under the material sun. However, our spiritual soul exists separate from material time, space, and matter. Therefore, the only way to bring something new into creation is through God's touch upon our submissive souls. Then, once a new, unique spiritual being is awakened from within our soul's void, our inner realm and creation's material realm may begin expressing our never-before-seen existence by using what has always existed.

Every material atom remains different. However, every material atom remains comparable to all other material atoms. Uniqueness, on the other hand, makes one incomparable. Once we exist as a unique spiritual being, then, as a never-before-seen world maker, we may orchestrate creation's differing atoms into a world approximating our uniqueness. Still, we do not make creation's atoms unique. Instead, we push and pull her toward temporarily expressing one who is unique.

If any atom ever attained our uniqueness, then it would instantly—and permanently—cease being a part of our mother's universal whole. God designed His world to always return to the forms He originally brought forth during the first seven days. At the same time, God also designed creation too flexibly and temporarily reorchestrate herself around each of His unique ones. As a result, creation is synchronously moving toward expressing the likeness of every human creator while simultaneously moving back toward expressing the likeness of her Creator.

God designed creation's atoms to work with every unique one. However, God also designed His world to prohibit anyone from becoming the Unique One by perpetually dismantling everything we make so Mother Nature might return to what He first made. When we interact with creation, every nearby atom will strain and strive toward expressing our uniqueness. However, since no atom may ever achieve our uniqueness, they cannot help but revert to the forms originally established by God. Although each atom of Mother Nature delights in pleasing everyone who is unlike anyone, she delights in pleasing no one like she does the Unique One.

A world maker touches creation to express how the Creator is touching them. Humanity's original design was to arouse creation to our world-making effort by offering her access to the World Maker by touching her as we've been touched by God. Consequently, any soul not resonating with the Creator's touch will cause creation to grow progressively disinterested in and dismissive toward their touch.

Actions, as the final form of inner co-creation, allow us to touch, shape, and breathe our uniqueness into God's world. The spiritual being who wears a customized mental image and emanates a customized emotional aura will craft a customized style of action with which to impress their unique likeness upon the material realm. Creation, like all feminine partners, is rather picky about who touches her. She expects us to court her and communicate with her because of our Father. Therefore, God's spiritual touch must resonate from our unique being, through our inner realm, and directly into her anatomical expanse. If she senses any disconnection between her Beloved's touch upon our soul and our body's touch upon her, she'll progressively withdraw from our world-making effort.

Creation—as a wholly material partner—cannot see, feel, or experience a spiritually unique one. Fortunately, the Creator designed the human mind, heart, and body to mentally depict, emotionally emanate, and physically express each one of His unique ones. Essentially, our mind, heart, and body vouch for our independent, authoritative uniqueness before creation. As fallen beings, we can only temporarily deceive our material mother into giving us access to her limitless orchestrational potential. However, after returning our soul to God so He might conceive a unique one from within our spiritual void, there is no longer a need for deception.

When creation sees thoughts, feels emotions, and experiences actions expressing one bearing their own likeness of Uniqueness, she'll not be able to resist obediently opening a portion of herself to the touch of our material body. Mother Nature wants us to touch her in a manner reminiscent of how our soul is being touched by God. As authoritative world makers, each of our fiery actions exists to touch, shape, and breathe our likeness of Uniqueness into God's world to bring forth our own unique world. Maintaining repetitious, intimate, and intense physical contact with creation's atoms is the only way to conceive, sustain, and innovate a unique world within God's world. The moment we stop touching creation's atoms, she'll immediately begin reverting those atoms back to the forms originally orchestrated by God.

First, each must be made into a unique world maker by God in His spiritual realm. Then, each must make their own image, aura, and style of action to approximate their world-making uniqueness amidst their inner realm. Finally, each must make a concerted and consistent effort to act upon creation to orchestrate their intended world. Our uniqueness must flow from God's touch into our soul, from our soul's touch into our body, and from our body's touch into creation. As long as our uniqueness is flowing forth from God's spiritual realm, through our inner realm, and into creation's material realm, our mother will delight in helping us orchestrate our world within her so she might continue growing toward becoming God's world of unique worlds.

Our Father does not want anyone touching our mother without the requisite reverence, respect, and recognition. While we're untouched souls, we don't actually touch creation because we do not even exist as spiritual beings of world-making authority. A fallen soul is spiritually non-existent, resulting in their body materially touching creation without authoritative direction. To our mother, being touched by a human form vacant of a living spiritual being is a disconcerting experience.

A spiritual being of world-making authority touches creation as an independent, authoritative, and unique world maker through their own mental image, emotional aura, and physical style of action customized to their likeness of Uniqueness. Being inseminated with the world-making intentions of a never-before-seen spiritual being is an exciting prospect for our mother. She doesn't know us or trust us. However, she knows and trusts the One touching us. Therefore, ensuring that we touch creation in a manner reminiscent of how God is touching our soul is vital for every orchestrational effort within the material realm.

Each level of progression from the Creator's spiritual realm and out through our inner realm is a stage that creation uses to gauge our growing competence as a creator. God is zealous for the purity of His world and for the development of His world makers. As a result, He created humanity as a progressive challenge for His unique ones. As we grow from God's spiritual realm, through our inner realm, and out into creation's material realm, we must display our independence, our authority, and our uniqueness at each stage of the ever-increasing challenge.

Spiritually submitting to God is an effortless act as He touches, shapes, and breathes His likeness into our souls to awaken a unique one. Then, mentally depicting our uniqueness is difficult. After that, summoning forth an emotional aura to constantly fill our sovereign sphere is taxing. Finally, animating our aura-imbued image to act in accordance with our unique spiritual being is borderline maddening. However, exerting a personal style of action upon creation to woo her with our touch of independent and authoritative uniqueness is the only way for a world maker to make a unique world within God's world.

When an unmarried individual inwardly develops their fiery style of actions, they'll be disadvantaged by not having anyone to practice those actions upon before unleashing them upon Mother Nature. A couple, in contrast, will have another world maker of light, water, and fire to refine their personal style of action with before having to learn the hard way with creation. A man, in particular, will benefit from the marital union by inwardly practicing his intended style of actions upon his feminine partner. Since his spouse embodies Mother Nature, inwardly exerting his style of actions upon her mind, heart, and body will give him a strong inclination of how things will go for him when he likewise begins touching God's world. A woman will also benefit by inwardly developing her personal style of action alongside her husband. Since her husband's aggressive mind, heart, and body are the primary instruments the couple will use to push their combined world-making intentions into God's world, developing her own style of action to seductively pull the couple's world-making intentions out through her partner's masculine mind, heart, and body will prepare her to do likewise with every unique one still held within the affectionate embrace of Mother Nature.

When a couple inwardly co-creates their two personalized styles of action, the initial experience is similar to the awkwardness that transpires when first engaging in sexual intercourse. The fumbling and bumbling inherent to authoritatively directing an aura-imbued image of masculinity to move in concert with an aura-imbued image of femininity is daunting. The goal is for each partner to create a personal style of action that allows both to move independently but toward one interconnected and interdependent end. Achieving such intertwined and personalized styles of action requires both sovereigns to have already co-created their two aura-imbued images together.

The couple who consciously direct their inner masculine and feminine likenesses toward acting in a sexual manner amidst their inner realm will elicit a strong compulsion for their bodies to do likewise in the material realm. However, the point of inner co-creation is to compel a totality of unified world-making actions, which includes—but is not limited to—sexual intercourse. A man's personal style of action exists to push the couple's combined world-making knowledge, desires, and intentions out into creation. Meanwhile, a woman's personal style of action exists to pull her husband and creation close so her partner's actions might successfully inseminate creation's atoms with the couple's world-making knowledge, desires, and intentions.

Each world maker's style of action is linked to the unique one within their soul. Understanding one's soul identity, creative expertise, principal purpose, seven uniques, and many other factors outlining one's likeness of Uniqueness will significantly influence the style of action one creates. Having a beneficially opposed partner within our inner realm to develop our actions with is vital for preparing a touch that will effectively inseminate Mother Nature. As a couple animates their two illuminated, flowing, and fiery forms, they'll start to sense how disconnected their past actions have been with their world-making intentions. Pushing and pulling creation toward making a unique world requires each partner's uniqueness to flow forth freely through both minds, hearts, and bodies before each of those inner stages of growth are cleared, and so material creation might open herself as the final stage of growth for the couple.

As a man and a woman become an independent, authoritative, and unique world-making union, every nearby couple, religious structure, and governmental institution will urgently pressure them toward conforming to pre-existing frameworks of marriage, masculinity, and femininity. However, each couple is responsible to co-create their own ways of thinking, feeling, and acting based exclusively upon their own spiritual relationship with their Creator. External authorities lead toward perfect replication, not unique orchestration. A couple's inner realm is under their spiritual authority. Therefore, any attempt to encroach, violate, or invade the marital sovereignty of two unique spiritual beings must be dealt with swiftly and severely.

The fewer external influences a couple allows into their inner realm, the more authoritative their thoughts, emotions, and actions will become. Authority flows from within, which is why external forces work so diligently to pressure humanity to conformity in their thoughts, emotions, and actions. Only by deceiving souls into surrendering their position of authority over their inner realm can external authorities even attempt to maintain control over the material realm.

The way a couple inwardly moves their masculine form upon their feminine form is based upon how each experiences God moving upon their soul. Likewise, the way a couple inwardly moves their feminine form, in response to their masculine form is based upon how both souls move in response to God. Therefore, the way both souls unite with God in the spiritual realm is the basis for how a couple unites in their inner realm, and the way a couple unites in their inner realm is the basis for how a couple's bodies unite in creation's material realm.

The challenge of conceiving, and then animating two inner world-makers composed of light, water, and fire cannot be understated. However, there is no other way to attain a visionary, meaningful, and purposeful existence. Each world maker is responsible for connecting the Creator's spiritual realm to creation's material realm through their inner realm. First, God spiritually makes us into a unique world maker. Then, we must make our own inner likeness of the unique world maker that God has already made. Finally, we may invest the inner world maker we've created so that—just as God did—our spiritual being might gain access to the material realm to make our own unique world.

Section 6
Material World Makers

Once two spiritual authorities unite as inner creators, they'll mentally, emotionally, and physically co-create the two inner world makers they need to make their own material world. Consequently, the male body expects a couple to lead him toward becoming a unique man, a unique creator, and, ultimately, a unique father. Similarly, a couple's female body expects a couple to lead her toward becoming a unique woman, a unique creation, and a unique mother. Then, as a world-making partnership uniquely embodies the first world-making partnership, a man will protectively push every world maker away from every other world maker to ensure a race of unique world makers, while a woman protectively pulls every world toward every other world to ensure a world of unique worlds.

Chapter 16
Man, Creator, Father

A male becomes a man the moment he takes it upon himself to approach the Unique One to become a unique one. Then, a man becomes a creator the moment he takes it upon himself to make his own unique world. And finally, a creator becomes a father the moment he takes it upon himself to make his own unique world in a way that will make the unique world makers that the World Maker desires.

A man is a unique one. A creator creates uniquely. And a father creates unique ones who create uniquely. Those who fail to lead their male body along its desired progression from a man into a creator before culminating in fatherhood will produce a demotivated, deplorable, and despised representation of masculinity. Unfortunately, any male body devoid of authoritative spiritual leadership will take it upon himself to ensure his own ascension to Perfection by destroying everything and everyone obstructing him from becoming the One.

Male bodies, while lacking their own unique spiritual authority, have no choice but to look to external authorities for guidance on how they might become a unique man, creator, and father. However, external authorities cannot lead a man toward uniqueness. External authorities can only lead a man toward the replication of pre-existing men, creators, and fathers. As a result, any man trained to think, feel, and act like other men—even the greatest of men—will grow bitter, wrathful, and enraged toward those who led him away from becoming a unique one.

Each man knows that becoming a replication of anyone will result in him becoming no one. Since uniqueness is the essence of masculinity, being made into a replication is a path that leads to a fate worse than death, an existence as one who does not even exist. Even if it were possible for a man to achieve the impossible by making himself into a perfect replication of the Man, the Creator, and the Father, he'd remain unable to shake his inexpressible despair at failing to be unique.

Only the Unique One may spiritually lead everyone toward becoming a unique one. Then, as a unique one, a spiritual being may lead their own mind, heart, and body toward inwardly and materially expressing their spiritual uniqueness. Technically, God could lead each male body toward thinking, feeling, and acting uniquely if He so desired. However, He does not, and He will not. The Creator desires to spiritually make unique ones who will then inwardly and materially make unique ones. God desires each soul to experience His greatest joy, making independent, authoritative, and unique world makers. Consequently, the fullest expression of uniqueness is neither being unique nor creating uniquely. The fullest expression of uniqueness is being unique, creating uniquely, and then creating unique ones who create uniquely. The male body is the instrument crafted by God to allow every soul—by birth or through the inner marital bond—to inwardly make a unique one who will materially make unique ones.

When it comes to a couple's co-creational efforts, the initial responsibility is leading their male mind, heart, and body away from any pre-existing forms of masculinity. Internal masculine orchestration may only begin once all forms of external masculine replication are removed. Once a man's mind, heart, and body are no longer looking to external authorities for leadership, a couple will find their male body looking expectantly toward them as his spiritual sovereigns.

Those not living in a faith-based, spiritual union with the Authority should not attempt to wrestle the allegiance of their male body away from external authorities. Since each untouched soul is a void of infinite emptiness, forcing a male body to express a vacuous one will bring about a rapid escalation in lawlessness, destruction, and violence as the male body works to turn his entire material environment into a domain suitable to one who is nothing, nowhere, and no one. Human societies have gone to great lengths to hedge in the frightening capabilities of the male body. Removing a male from the social structures designed to limit the destructive nature of unguided masculinity is extremely dangerous. Obligating a masculine body to only follow the leadership of a soul who is nothing, nowhere, and no one will result in the ever-increasing probability of unrestrained masculine aggression.

Only those living in a faith-based, spiritual union with the Authority are being touched, shaped, and breathed into a unique spiritual authority capable of effectively leading a male body. However, spiritual leadership, as God demonstrates in His union with each soul, is not achieved through decree or dictatorship but through being. As a result, a couple must not attempt to lead their embodiment of masculinity by dictating to him how he should think, feel, and act. Creating unique ways of thinking, feeling, and acting is the job of the male mind, heart, and body. Instead, as spiritual beings, we exert the purest form of authoritative leadership—being.

Being one who is unlike anyone is how we lead creation. Our orchestrational mother delights in reorganizing her atoms to materially express each one of God's unique ones. Therefore, a couple leads their male body away from looking, feeling, and acting like any pre-existing form of masculinity to ensure that he'll shape his masculine thoughts, emotions, and actions toward expressing their spiritual uniqueness. Once a male body can mentally see, emotionally feel, and physically experience two united and unique ones—who are each unlike anyone—he'll then begin making his own unique ways of thinking, feeling, and acting so he might uniquely express his sovereigns' authoritative uniqueness.

Each male body is mired in despair at being unable to find his own exclusive source of authoritative uniqueness. Men look to their fathers, their idols, and their ancestors for inspiration, only to drown amidst a life of replication. However, the moment a unique spiritual being—or two unique spiritual beings—appear miraculously from within him, a male body will eagerly begin shaping his thoughts, emotions, and actions toward expressing his newfound source of uniqueness. Still, what the male body then produces will not be a perfect replication of the spiritual sovereigns within him. Instead, he'll form his own material ways of expressing those who inwardly lead him so that he might become his own independent, authoritative, and unique world-making creator.

The masculine mental image, emotional aura, and physical style of action that a couple creates amidst their shared inner realm are the triune connection that will conduct their authority in the spiritual realm, through their shared inner realm, and out into creation's material realm. A couple's male body innately desires to exert material authority but understands that he must receive his authority from someone who is an authority. Therefore, a male body will commit to any being capable of leading him toward making his own form of authoritative uniqueness. The masculine image, aura, and style of action a couple forms within their shared inner realm is how both sovereigns inwardly anoint their male mind, heart, and body with their authoritative likeness so that he might adaptively exert their united spiritual authority out into the ever-changing complexities of Mother Nature.

As a male body follows the authoritative leadership emanating from his spiritual authorities, he'll strive to lead humanity toward being a race of unique world makers. A male body wants to be made into a unique one so that he, too, might make unique ones. This natural process of personally motivated perpetuation is of God's design. The Masculine Creator wants each man to bear and exert the fullness of His world-making likeness by becoming a maker of unique world makers.

A unique man creates a unique world so that he might materially sustain the making of unique world makers. The most obvious opportunity for a male developing into a man, a creator, and a father is biological reproduction. Conceiving a child provides a couple with an intimate opportunity to participate in the original and still functioning world-making union between our spiritual Father and our material mother. When biological conception takes place, God weaves one of His precious spiritual souls into one of creation's treasured material bodies. As the embodiment of creation, a woman has the honor of carrying the spiritual world maker until their inner realm is sufficiently developed for the material realm. Then, after birth, a woman intuitively lifts the fully formed triune world maker toward her husband. As the embodiment of the Father, a man is expected to take charge of the child's development into a fully independent, authoritative, and unique world maker.

When a child is born, a man brings the new world maker into his world, which, like God's world, is custom designed to make world makers. A father's foremost charge is to ensure the spiritual development of the child. At the same time, a mother's foremost charge is to ensure the material development of the child. As a couple, both spouses work together to ensure the inner development of the child. The Creator and creation expect each child entrusted to a couple's care to be fully matured into a spiritual sovereign, inner creator, and material world maker before they're permitted to venture forth into God's world to make their world.

A man will find that mentally depicting a minuscule sovereign sphere within a child's body will help him measure the growth of the inexperienced world maker's authority. When first born, a child's sphere of sovereignty does not even encapsulate their own body since they remain unable to direct their own thoughts, emotions, and actions. However, as a child's spiritual authority grows, a father will see that development as the slow expansion of their sovereign sphere. Similar to how our spiritual Father and material mother relinquish their authority over us as we grow, so a father and a mother must slowly relinquish their authority over a child as the growing sovereign's authority expands.

Although biologically conceiving, developing, and releasing a fully mature, triune world maker into God's world is the most obvious example of a man's development into a father, every male seeks to attain an even broader patriarchal influence. A self-defining authority develops into a co-defining authority so that he might become a global-defining authority. Each male desires to exert a broad father-like influence upon mankind. However, a male body does not desire to father humanity the way the Father does. Instead, each male body desires to create his own unique way of fathering humanity while allowing God to father humanity in His own unique way.

Some consider any man with a broad reach of authority as inherently evil. However, the scope of a man's influence is neither good nor evil. The goodness of man's authority is based upon whether he intends to make himself into the Authority or make everyone—including himself—into a unique authority.

Chapter 17
Woman, Creation, Mother

A female becomes a woman once she takes it upon herself to attract a unique one to make a unique world with her. A woman then becomes an embodiment of feminine creation once she takes it upon herself to attract each unique one to make their own unique world alongside her unique world. And finally, an embodiment of feminine creation becomes a mother once she takes it upon herself to attract every unique one—and their unique world—toward bringing forth one interconnected world of unique worlds.

A fallen female never becomes a unique woman, a unique creation, or a unique mother because she is still trying to become the woman, the creation, and the mother. Fallen women cannot attract the Unique One, or even a unique one, because they refuse to submissively, obediently, and affectionately express anyone else's uniqueness. Instead, a fallen woman uses the irresistible allure of her feminine mind, heart, and body to attract everyone and everything to serve her as the world of unique worlds.

A fallen female's vindictiveness toward a man, all humanity, and ultimately God arises from being born untouched, unwanted, and unloved by the Man, the Creator, and the Father. Such an unalterable judgment of spiritual undesirability impels every fallen woman to pull herself into a position of equality with God so she might enact justice upon Him. However, each fallen woman will ultimately fail to attract anyone as long as her soul remains spiritually undesirable. What a fallen woman cannot accept is that her soul's present untouched state of infinite spiritual emptiness is what makes her an irresistible spiritual virgin to Infinite Fullness. Therefore, until a woman submissively surrenders her soul—as the spiritual virgin she already is—she'll never know the touch of Desire marking her as His uniquely desirable one.

Exposing the spiritual intent of every fallen female to take every world and make herself into God's world of unique worlds also reveals how every woman is misusing feminine submission. A fallen soul housed within a feminine body will feign material submission to bring a man close to her authoritative soul. Then, once she's brought a man close enough, she'll take his world, position, and identity. As a result, each fallen woman uses material submission to enable her spiritual elevation.

Our mother modeled feminine submission during the first seven days. Instead of submitting so she could make herself, creation submitted so her Beloved could make her. Fallen women do follow the first premise of creation's example, but they do not trust the One who has already left them untouched, unloved, and unascended. Therefore, each fallen woman takes the responsibility for her ascension upon herself. Conversely, when a soul submits before the Masculine Creator, they look only to His touch for their ascension into their own likeness of His uniqueness. Then, once God has made a living spiritual sovereign, the unique one may turn toward their mind, heart, and body with the expectation of submission so they might impart their own uplifting touch of uniqueness.

A couple makes their female body into a unique woman, creation, and mother as she submits to them as her spiritual authorities. Likewise, a couple makes their male body into a unique man, creator, and father as he also submits to them as his spiritual authorities. Then, the couple's male body will push the world-making intentions of both souls into their female body to make her into the mother of their unique world. After all, God designed the partnership between the male and female bodies to enable each marital partnership to uniquely do what the first partnership did during the first seven days.

When two sovereigns—touched by the Sovereign—start leading their female body, they must not demand their female mind, heart, and body submit to their male mind, heart, and body. Material bodies may only submit to spiritual sovereigns. A male body submits to both souls by forming aggressive thoughts, emotions, and actions that will push the couple's spiritual world-making intentions out into the material realm. At the same time, a female body submits to both souls by forming submissive thoughts, emotions, and actions that will help pull the couple's spiritual world-making intentions out through the male body and into her as the couple's embodiment of Mother Nature.

Leading one another's bodies toward expressing what both souls are experiencing with God requires an intimate inner partnership. After all, a woman's body will always remain loyal to her own soul. If a female body senses her masculine partner is misusing her submissive offerings, then she'll withdraw from his touch to protect the sovereignty of her soul. Then, the couple's world will begin to crumble. As the embodiment of creation, a woman's body is intimately interconnected with Mother Nature. As a result, the way a wife reacts to the touch of her husband will reverberate through creation's atoms to engender either increased submission or increased rejection. Therefore, if a couple desires to orchestrate their own world within God's world, then ensuring their male body is pushing their combined world-making intentions into the waiting embrace of their female body is essential for ensuring a fertile insemination of the first feminine partner.

For millennia, men have been deceiving, manipulating, and forcing the submission of female bodies in the hope that they might compel creation to do likewise. Mother Nature looks expectantly to each woman for cues regarding which men she should submissively open herself to. Creation intuitively knows that the way a man treats his foremost feminine partner is also how he'll treat her as the foremost feminine partner.

In the beginning, the Masculine Creator proclaimed everything that the first feminine partner brought forth on His behalf as good. Conversely, a fallen man will never proclaim anything that any feminine partner brings forth on his behalf as good. Creation and women submit so they might know and express their masculine partner. Unfortunately, amidst our present fallen age, that means that every act of feminine submission will provide creation, or woman, with the unpleasant experience of knowing and expressing a lightless, loveless, and lifeless soul living amidst the delusion of being the One who is Light, Love, and Life. Consequently, the resulting material expressions displaying a man's spiritually vacuous soul will not please any man intent on maintaining his delusion of being the Man.

Even the slightest act of submission by a female body will result in her knowing and expressing both her husband's soul and her own soul. A couple who wishes to lead their feminine body toward any act of submission must face this inevitability. Also, the male body must be led to understand that his feminine partner's expressions are not about him but the spiritual beings within. A co-created effort by both spiritual authorities will be required to lead a female body toward intimately partnering with a male body. Then, both souls will need to embrace holistic responsibility for all that arises from their female body so that their male body may genuinely express gratitude, delight, and love toward the goodness of all his feminine partners' expressions.

All a woman's expressions, like creation, will span the full spectrum of anatomical possibilities, which are all designed to materially approximate spiritual beings. Unfortunately, even for resurrected souls, the taker's likeness will remain. As a result, every expression a woman or creation brings forth will simultaneously display the resurrected nature of both spiritual beings and the still lingering fallen nature of both spiritual beings. Therefore, hidden horrors will linger within all a couple's moments of bliss, ecstasy, and euphoria, while hidden hopes will linger within all a couple's moments of suffering, strife, and horror.

As material objects, both the male and the female bodies are good. Furthermore, all the anatomical thoughts, emotions, and actions that both bodies produce are also always good. The only thing that is not good are souls living spiritually separate from the One who is Good. As a result, when two sovereigns embrace holistic responsibility for every material expression rising through their bodies, they free both bodies to continue their always good world-making union without having to judge the goodness or evil of what they're materially producing. Since the Spiritual Authority has already judged all material creation as good, all resurrected spiritual authorities must do likewise. The deeper assessments of spiritual knowledge, desire, and intent must be kept between both sovereigns to impel their ever-increasing submission before the Masculine Creator. Then, the couple's material bodies may simply continue expressing both sovereigns' growing spiritual development through their always good world-making union with one another.

When a female body is touched, shaped, and breathed into by her masculine partner, she'll bring forth robust expressions of who both souls are together as co-creating spiritual authorities. A fallen man rejects all these expressions out of hand as falling short of his delusional perception of his own perfection. Any attempt by any man to alter any feminine expression is an attempt to alter the material expressions of his spiritual being in the hope that doing so will simultaneously alter his spiritual being. However, the only alteration required lies in the spiritual being of the man's soul and the woman's soul. Then, as both souls turn afresh to be touched, shaped, and breathed into by the Soulmate, their two minds, hearts, and bodies will simply continue materially expressing their spiritual growth as united world-making authorities.

Creation is complex. As the embodiment of creation, a woman's expressive work is always holistically inclusive. Consequently, each feminine expression is designed by her body to facilitate interconnection between everything and everyone amidst the entire universal world of unique worlds. Anything less than a man's wholehearted embrace of everything a woman brings forth will shatter her efforts to ensure everything they create is ideally prepared for interconnection with every world and every world maker within God's world of unique worlds. Therefore, a couple must train their male body to delight in every expression rising from their female body to ensure their world remains ideally prepared for global interconnection.

We learn from God how He is the Masculine Creator and how we are His feminine creation. Then, we direct our masculine and feminine forms to do likewise. Still, a man, in particular, will assume that failing to replicate God's touch upon his soul, in how he touches his wife, is a failure. However, a male body is not designed to touch a female body the way God touches anyone's soul. Each masculine one must exert a touch that is unlike anyone, including unlike God. As a result, each female body wants to help her chosen masculine partner develop his own unique way of touching her so that he might uniquely touch creation in a way that will engender their unique world.

A woman pulls one male toward her body so that, together, they might make their own unique world. However, as a female begins to recognize herself as a woman, she'll start aching for a more robust embodiment of femininity. Consequently, the woman determined to continue her development will expand her alluring nature and begin pulling on everyone. However, as an embodiment of feminine creation, a woman does not pull anyone—other than her husband—toward her body. Instead, she pulls each world maker toward their portion of the material realm. A robust embodiment of feminine creation arouses each soul to unite with creation's atoms as if she is those atoms. Such a woman aches for each unique one to inseminate Mother Nature with their spiritual world-making intentions so she may help creation—as the one who embodies creation—become God's world of unique worlds.

Unsurprisingly, fallen men react poorly when their chosen feminine partner starts arousing, embracing, and enabling everyone as a world-making creator. After all, a fallen man wants to be the One and Only Creator. Therefore, fallen men use their bodies to bemoan, belittle, and beat their feminine spouse to keep her from arousing anyone to world-making other than him. A married couple is responsible for making sure their male body does not stifle the expanding allure of their female body before she can mature into a global-pulling authority. The scope of allure emanating from an irresistible woman is neither good nor evil. Instead, the goodness of an irresistible woman depends upon whether she's attracting every human creator to unite with her or with our orchestrational mother.

Fallen men do not understand and do not react well to their feminine partner exerting a global attraction. Each fallen man wants to be the One and Only Masculine Creator upon which his wife and all feminine partners pull. The male propensity for promiscuity is based upon each man's desire to be the One worshiped by the entire whole of universal femininity. Still, every female body rightfully desires to seductively arouse every unique one to conceive, sustain, and innovate their own unique world within God's world.

The female body sees no point in making a distinction between her embodiment of feminine creation and the universal whole of Mother Nature. A woman wants to excite every soul to touch creation's atoms with the same unbridled passion her body arouses from her husband and her soul arouses from God. Only a man committed to exerting a global push in leading all toward becoming a race of unique world makers will recognize the goodness of his feminine partner's commitment to exerting a global pull in leading all toward making a world of unique worlds.

A female becomes a unique woman as she pulls one man close to her body so that, together, they might orchestrate their own unique world. Then, a woman becomes a unique embodiment of feminine creation as she pulls every soul close to creation so each might orchestrate their own unique world. Still, even amidst such an exultant embodiment of irresistibility, a woman will remain restless as she presses on toward the fullest embodiment of femininity as a mother. Developing into an orchestrational mother—who uniquely embodies the orchestrational mother—requires a woman to do more than simply arouse each creator to create their own unique world within God's world. An orchestrational mother authoritatively oversees all humanity's world-making efforts to ensure every world is growing in an interconnected manner that synchronously, simultaneously, and equally benefits the Creator, creation, and every human creator.

Every woman strives toward being a unique orchestrational mother muddied only by her efforts toward becoming the orchestrational mother. An example of how all women intuitively pursue motherhood lies in their relentless hunger to know everything about everyone. The female body assumes that gathering such information will be used by her soul to oversee the mutually beneficial growth of every world within God's world. Over time though, each female body discovers that no one, including her own soul, is interested in the foremost desire of creation.

Pulling all human creators toward a global partnership that will synchronously, simultaneously, and equally fulfill everyone's world-making intentions is a task that only an orchestrational mother may achieve. The woman who matures fully into an orchestrational mother is a living epicenter of allure who is actively pulling every world toward every other world so that, together, all might interconnect into one world of unique worlds. Each woman's body yearns to radiate a level of attraction so irresistible that the Creator, creation, and all human creators come to her to reform the original world-making partnership.

A woman is the original mediator between humanity and creation. A woman's alluring nature melts through everyone's resistance to co-creational partnerships despite all the wrongs, hurt feelings, and broken promises. Creation is angry at humanity, and humanity feels betrayed by creation. However, the woman who is an epicenter of irresistible attraction will pull everyone together so that all might begin moving forward in oneness toward making the world of unique worlds that all desire.

A couple directs their male body toward becoming a unique man, a unique creator, and a unique father so he might mediate between humanity and the Creator. Then, a couple directs their female body toward becoming a unique woman, a unique creation, and a unique mother so she might mediate between humanity and creation. Then, as a man and a woman, as a creator and creation, and as a father and a mother, a couple may lead all toward becoming an independent, interconnected, and interdependent race of unique world makers who, together, are bringing forth a world of unique worlds.

Chapter 18
The Protectors of Uniqueness

The couple who leads their male body toward becoming a unique man, creator, and father and their female body toward becoming a unique woman, creation, and mother will provide humanity with the two authorities required for protecting everyone's uniqueness. A man of unstoppable aggression will push everyone apart so each might become a unique one amidst one race of unique world makers. At the same time, a woman of irresistible submission will pull every world together so that all might unite into one world of unique worlds. Although the male body is traditionally recognized as the protector, that is only because his protective efforts are far more obvious in contrast to the far more subtle methods of the feminine protector.

The classic depiction of protection is a male interposing himself between a violent aggressor and a helpless victim. Through the use of mental, emotional, and physical repulsion, a male body may push back against an aggressor. Masculine protection exists to ensure that no one's soul, body, or world is forcibly conformed into the likeness of any other. Whenever a male body sees, feels, or experiences encroachments, violations, or invasions upon the sovereign sphere of another, his likeness of the One—who is Anger, Wrath, and Violence—will awaken to unleash anger, wrath, and violence upon the aggressor.

As a couple starts leading their male body toward aggressively protecting every soul's sovereignty, they'll uncover deep-rooted hesitation. Amidst the present age of world takers, no one wants to deal with masculine bodies obstructing them from becoming the One over everyone. Therefore, all societies collectively constrain young men to stunt their masculine development. Since everyone is trying to encroach, violate, and invade every else's world, keeping male bodies apathetic, incompetent, and unresponsive is of the highest priority. Unfortunately, since every male body must express its likeness to the One who is Anger, Wrath, and Violence, when those undirected expressions do arise, they tend to appear in forms that only reinforce society's claim that masculinity must be crushed.

Even governments tremble before the male embodiment of the Masculine Creator. When preparing for war, an aggressive government will go to great lengths to avoid arousing the anger, wrath, and violence of the males in an enemy's lands while simultaneously arousing the anger, wrath, and violence of the males in their lands. A government intent on aggression will claim historical injustices, assert treaty violations, or even stage a fake incursion to make themselves appear like the victim before they invade. Such devious efforts exist to enrage the males of their country while shaming the males of an enemy country.

Curiously, the amount of anger, wrath, and violence a male body exudes is inversely proportional to the scope of the injustice. If a man sees his country being invaded by an aggressor, he might fight passionately but nowhere near the full scope of his capabilities for masculine fury. However, if a man sees his wife being forcibly invaded by an aggressor, then he'll redefine the very essence of masculine fury. Consequently, the male body is not designed to protect the sovereignty of states but the sovereignty of souls.

As a male matures into a unique man, creator, and father, he'll find his protective instincts expanding beyond his spouse, his children, and his community toward everyone loved by the Unique One. Still, his capacity for masculine protection will remain awakened only by the violation of individual sovereignty. Governments attempt to bridge this disconnect by making crude comparisons, such as equating the violation of a nation as being equal to the violation of a home, wife, and children.

However, such abstractions do not translate effectively. Every male body remains committed to protecting the sovereignty of souls and not the states that routinely violate the sovereignty of souls.

The Masculine Creator is the Protector. However, if the Infinite One ever exerted His protective nature within the finite material realm, then He'd inevitably encroach, violate, and invade everyone's sovereignty. Above all, God desires to make independent, authoritative, and unique world makers, making any of His direct exertions of authority within the material realm an unmitigated threat to every world maker's sovereignty. As a result, God made the finite male body to materially protect the sovereignty, individuality, and liberty of His unique ones. Unfortunately, once the first man rebelled, all men lost their original position of material authority over creation, which negated all men as masculine protectors. Fortunately, God came as the Man to reclaim that authority and offer to any man the opportunity of returning to the likeness of the Protector.

Everyone is rightfully frightened by a male body operating outside the control of external authorities. We fear this because we instinctively know that no spiritual authority exists within any male body. As a result, everyone expects only one thing from a man operating free from external control. Still, the fearsome potential laden within a man's anger, wrath, and violence is not evil. When a spiritual authority—or two in the case of marriage—directs those elements properly, the result will be the forceful obstruction of everyone attempting to get into a position of authority over anyone. Each soul touched by the Authority becomes a spiritual authority capable of inwardly leading a male body away from any form of external control and toward protecting everyone from any form of external control.

A foundational principle for leading a male body toward exerting masculine protection is to use thoughts when dealing with spiritual children, use emotions when dealing with spiritual adolescents, and use

143

actions when dealing with spiritual adults. A spiritual child is someone who still sees God's world as their world. For such inexperienced creators, a man will mentally push a clear depiction of their sovereign sphere, his sovereign sphere, and every creator's sovereign sphere into the child's mind. When a man's mental work is complete, the spiritual child will be able to see the illuminated outline of every creator's world alongside their world. If a spiritual child decides to willfully cross the illuminated lines demarcating the sovereignty of another, then a man will stop dealing with them as a spiritual child and start dealing with them as a spiritual adolescent.

A spiritual adolescent is a soul who mentally sees the sovereign domain of every world maker but remains determined to see how much they can take. When a masculine protector recognizes this effort, he'll respond by exerting an aura of emotional repulsion to push their soul back from the sovereign domain they desire to violate. Most can recall a moment in their youth when a father or a father figure caught them crossing a line and glared at them from across the room in a manner that filled them with terror. The emotional fury that a masculine heart emanates is an unmistakable experience for adolescents. However, if a spiritual adolescent does not retreat before a man's emotional warning, then he'll begin dealing with them as a spiritual adult.

A spiritual adult is a soul who mentally sees the sovereignty of every creator, invades the world of another anyway, and does not retreat before a masculine protector's emotional warning. Spiritual adults respect only one thing: force. If they are not dealt with in a swift and aggressive manner, then they'll rapidly grow into a full-fledged taker intent on helping themselves to everything and everyone until there is only one. Therefore, a masculine protector uses his actions against invasive spiritual adults to physically remove them from the sovereign domain of another, as well as instruct everyone present about the purpose of masculinity.

A taker's temerity is based upon their personal delusion of Perfection. When someone sees themselves as the Superior One, they sense it is not only their option to subjugate others but their obligation. It is for such beings that a male body must direct the full potential of his fury. Still, every protective action that a man unleashes will have significant consequences and must be customized to the scale of the mental encroachment, emotional violation, or physical invasion.

A complimentary principle for a male body in unleashing his protective actions is to always exert masculine aggression just one magnitude higher than the taker. For example, if a taker reaches into another's world, then a masculine creator might grab their hand. If the taker seizes something from within another's world, then a masculine creator might grab their hand, trip them, and take them to the ground. However, if a taker attacks another's body—with the clear intent to harm—then a masculine creator might grab them, slam them to the ground, and knock them out cold. The intent of such aggressive actions is to communicate to the taker and anyone else present that violating the sovereignty of another will always be rebuffed with one magnitude of force beyond what was used for invasion. Without masculine creators exercising such protective thoughts, emotions, and actions on the behalf of every soul, then the nature of the taker within all of us will run rampant to destroy everyone's sovereignty, individuality, and liberty.

As a couple leads their male body toward thinking, feeling, and acting protectively, they'll naturally puzzle over how he might have a sufficiency of authority to repulse any invasive effort. Many men prepare themselves as protectors by mentally, emotionally, and physically training for combative situations. Although training is useful, such capabilities are used to exert authority, not generate authority. The only way to generate the authority needed to exert limitless material authority is to be a spiritual authority.

A spiritual being is the source of all human authority. Consequently, every male body lacks confidence in his ability to repulse invasive threats because he's never met the Authority. Therefore, a spiritual authority—created by the Authority—must exist before a male body can exert masculine protection with confidence. The couple who desires their male body to protect the independence, uniqueness, and world-making opportunity of every soul must be the spiritual authorities their male body draws upon to exert his repulsive, masculine protection.

Existing as a spiritual being of anger, wrath, and violence only arrives after a soul has been touched by the One who is Anger, Wrath, and Violence. Additionally, one must remember that God—as the Infinite One—is indivisible. Therefore, anyone touched by the One who is the Source of Everything awakens into one who may uniquely express Light, Love, Life, Truth, Compassion, Mercy, Judgment, Anger, Wrath, Violence and all the other incomprehensible attributes of the Source. Once a couple recognizes that their male body needs their spiritual authority to act as a protective material authority, then they'll begin touching, shaping, and breathing into their male body to make him into their masculine protector of uniqueness.

Untouched souls hope that thinking, feeling, and acting like an authority will make them into the Authority. However, all such attempts will fail because materially looking, feeling, and acting like an authority cannot make one into the spiritual Authority. Furthermore, untouched souls depend upon material objects for their authority. As a result, when those material objects inevitably move, an untouched soul's facade of authority vanishes. Only human bodies anchored to their own unique spiritual being of authority will have no need to rely upon external representations of authority. Once a couple anchors their male body to their spiritual existence—which exists outside of time, space, and matter—a man will find he may exert bursts of aggressive repulsion that cut across time, space, and matter to separate creators from creation and souls from bodies. A masculine protector, anchored to and expressing two unique spiritual authorities, is an unstoppable sword against world takers and an impenetrable shield for world makers.

It is now time to put aside the obvious and aggressive nature of masculine protection so we might ponder the subtle and submissive nature of feminine protection. A male's obvious forms of protection are focused on guarding unique world makers. However, a female's subtle forms of protection are focused on guarding unique worlds. A masculine protector pushes apart every unique world maker, while a feminine protector pulls together every unique world. As a couple, a man and a woman protect what our Father and our mother treasure most.

The feminine creation exists to help every spiritual being create their own unique world within her as God's world of unique worlds. A female body develops by helping one man make a unique world, helping each one make their own unique world, and finally helping everyone make a world of unique worlds. The couple who desires to lead their female body along this path must allow her to extend her alluring nature toward becoming a global epicenter of orbital attraction so that she might pull every nearby world together into one world of unique worlds.

A woman's ability to protect every world begins by pulling the world-making intentions of her soul and her spouse's soul out through her male partner. As both souls meld their world-making intentions together amidst their shared inner realm, their male body will push, and their female body will pull that world-making mystery out into the material realm. The stronger a woman's mental, emotional, and physical pull upon her spouse, the more she helps her two spiritual sovereigns attain the actualization of their world-making intentions. As a woman grows confident in her ability to help her husband in delivering their world-making intentions out into Mother Nature, she'll start to sense how she might assist every other world maker do likewise.

The female body is passionate about avoiding perfect replication and ensuring unique orchestration. For example, when a female body receives her husband's genetic material, she forms a child, but in a way that synthesizes her husband's traits, her traits, their parents' traits, their ancestors' traits, the Masculine Creator's traits, the feminine creation's traits, and the traits of anyone else who might prove relevant to the child's eventual world-making effort. The female body integrates traits during a child's gestation to prepare the new sovereign for a seamless interconnection with every world and every world maker amidst God's world. In fact, it was the woman's propensity for elegant integration that preserved the Masculine Creator's traits across generations of human beings so that He might enter the material realm through her and reclaim the first man's vacated position of authority over creation. A female body performs this same service with everything she creates, both with her husband and with every other world maker.

As an embodiment of the world of unique worlds, a feminine protector works to ensure every world is growing toward global interconnection. Her service, although subtle and often overlooked, is a protective act because it ensures that everyone has a stake in everyone else's world. Then, anyone who invades any world will arouse the anger, wrath, and violence of everyone who holds a stake within that world.

A woman pulls one masculine creator toward her material body. A robust embodiment of feminine creation pulls every world maker toward their portion of the natural world. And a mother pulls every world closer to every other world so that all worlds within her orbital allure might grow into one interconnected world of unique worlds.

When a woman touches a man, she'll arouse him to push the couple's world-making intentions into her. When a feminine creation touches another creator, she'll arouse them to push their world-making intentions into their personal portion of the natural world. And when a mother touches all creators, she'll arouse each to present her with their world-making intentions so she might implant them inside every world within her world of unique worlds.

A woman who embodies our mother will represent humanity before creation. Men and children have an inexhaustible capacity for angering our orchestrational mother. A woman may glean leniency from Mother Nature to the benefit of all. When standing before creation, a woman seductively pulls our mother back toward her original union with humanity to provide creation—and herself—with the world of unique worlds they both desire.

When dealing with spiritual children, adolescents, and adults, a woman's protection is just as effective as a man's. Sometimes masculine repulsion is simply not the right tool for the job. Consequently, a woman's power over takers is not dependent upon how aggressively she pushes them out of another's sovereign domain. Instead, her protective power is based upon her ability to seductively pull creation's atoms away from an aggressive soul—which includes a taker's own mind, heart, and body.

It is easy to forget that a taker is simply an untouched spiritual soul temporarily encased inside a material form. Consequently, a woman does not push the mind, heart, and body of a taker away but pulls them toward herself and away from the untouched soul within. Fallen beings are misguiding, mistreating, and mutilating creation's atoms to force Mother Nature to do their bidding. An enraged mother channels the wrath of creation by exuding a touch upon another's mind, heart, and body that threatens to tear the mistreated atoms away from their spiritual abuser. A mother's touch profoundly threatens the fallen being within by reminding them of how precarious their position remains as long as they persist in depending upon creation's material atoms for their spiritual ascension into Perfection.

When dealing with a spiritual child, a feminine protector pulls their mind away from their taking-tactics by implanting a spectacular mental image of what she envisions for their world amidst her world of unique worlds. Should the taker persist, a woman will then deal with them as a spiritual adolescent by pulling them into her complex, intoxicating, and overwhelming emotional aura to saturate a taker's heart with an irresistible desire to be a part of her world of unique worlds. If they still rebuff her, a mother will treat the aggressor like a spiritual adult by touching them with a level of attraction so irresistible that she'll begin peeling the atoms of their mind, heart, and body away from their soul so the untouched one within might see, feel, and experience what awaits them should they continue to spurn the mother of the living.

A feminine protector must beware of the temptation inherent to pulling the atoms of another's mind, heart, and body toward herself. For example, many men have experienced a relationship with a woman where they have felt trapped. A man in such a relationship literally cannot mentally see, emotionally feel, or physically attempt to escape because his feminine partner has subtly pulled the atoms of his mind, heart, and body away from obeying his soul and toward obeying only her soul. Although this is initially dire for the man, over the long term, such an effort destroys the feminine nature of a woman's body who—like creation—is designed to help every creator make their world, not enslave every creator to her.

Like the male body, every female body harbors a deep-rooted hesitation toward forcefully exerting her protective nature. Still, if a couple intends to be a father and a mother for humanity, then they'll need their female body freely and confidently expanding her capacity for irresistibility. Leading our species toward becoming a race of unique world makers who are bringing forth a world of unique worlds requires a man pushing everyone apart while a woman pulls everything together.

A mother weaves every world together by arousing every creator's desire to make their world into the most important world within her world of unique worlds. The woman who performs this service will need to employ submissive subtlety so that no one realizes how she is seeding everyone's domain with the world-making intentions of every world maker. Those blessed by a mother's touch will discover—to their amazement—that everything growing within their world will prove inexplicably essential to every nearby world maker's world. Likewise, every nearby world maker will also be creating exactly what their world needs. A mother's work must remain subtle because God demands that each of His unique ones must remain free from external manipulation so all might develop into His race of independent, authoritative, and unique world makers. However, like creation, a woman knows that the material atoms around each spiritual sovereign need a mother's touch to guide them toward becoming a world of interconnected worlds.

A mother's effect is similar to how redwood trees intertwine their roots so that each might attain a height together that none could achieve individually. However, her leadership is material, not spiritual. A mother's nurturing effect is upon the material atoms, not the spiritual creators. As a couple, a father sees to the spiritual independence of every world maker, while a mother sees to the material interconnection of their worlds. Together, a couple ensures that all world makers and their worlds are growing progressively more interdependent.

Most of a mother's work will remain intuitive. However, as an authoritative world-maker, a woman retains her individual authority by always keeping her body at the center of her orchestrational efforts. Consequently, whenever a mother enters another world maker's world, her physical presence temporarily makes that world the epicenter of her world of unique worlds. Such a blessing, although temporary, may be extended. Should a mother desire, her presence may arouse all the atoms within another world maker's world and direct them toward submissively serving their world maker with a passion akin to the way she submissively serves the World Maker.

When an orchestrational mother enters another's world, she'll be ushered in like a queen visiting a foreign realm. What will not be obvious to those she visits is what her alluring presence pulls in behind her. Behind an irresistible embodiment of creation is an orchestrational river carrying the world-making intentions of every world maker within her world of unique worlds. However, the river behind a mother is moving toward her—not away from her—thereby drawing in and saturating every world she visits with the world-making intentions of every world maker she's touched. If a man attempted to initiate such an incursion of foreign world-making intentions, then he'd be thrown out. However, an irresistible woman, who subtly embodies intuitive creation and lives as a mother of orchestrational order, is able to achieve what no man should even consider attempting.

The woman who embodies our orchestrational mother knows that the best way to protect the uniqueness of every world is to inseminate every world with the world-making intentions of every world maker. A man cannot provide this type of protective service. A man's leadership is too obvious and aggressive. Only a woman may ensure the cross-pollination of all worlds to make sure every world is interconnected with—and protective over—every other world.

Mother Nature is exclusively material and intuitive. However, a woman is more complex. A woman is both spiritually authoritative and materially intuitive. As a result, a woman's body will intuitively cross-pollinate every world while her soul exerts a more directly authoritative touch. Therefore, the woman who is dedicated, defiant, and determined enough to become a unique orchestrational mother for humanity will hone the high art of authoritatively crafting a mother's seed. Crafting a mother's seed requires a woman to distill the essence of every creator's world-making knowledge, desires, and intentions and then combine them all into one mental, emotional, and physical seed, thereby encapsulating the world of unique worlds she's growing. As a result, whenever a mother touches a creator, she'll plant this seed inside their mind, heart, and body so that they, too, might begin to see, feel, and experience the world of unique worlds that she's bringing forth. Additionally, an orchestrational mother may also augment her seed so that each creator she touches will begin to see, feel, and experience how she desires their world to operate as the centerpiece of her world of unique worlds.

As a mother's seed develops inside a creator's world, each sovereign will slowly start to realize how their world is independent of every other world, interconnected with every other world, and interdependent on every other world within her world of unique worlds. The euphoria inherent to seeing, feeling, and experiencing one's world holding together all worlds is a subtle way of leading everyone away from taking and toward world-making. Then, anyone intent on taking from any world must imperil their opportunity to make the most important world within the entirety of God's world of unique worlds.

A mother knows that the best way to protect everyone's uniqueness is to pull every world together to form one world of unique worlds. A father knows that the best way to protect everyone's uniqueness is to push every world maker apart to form one race of unique world makers. Together, a father and a mother are the two protectors humanity needs to ensure the sovereignty, individuality, and liberty of everyone and everything within the World Maker's world.

Part 3
A Global-Defining Authority

A man becomes a self-defining authority to make one world-making creator. Then, a man becomes a co-defining authority to make two world-making creators. Finally, a man becomes a global-defining authority to make everyone a world-making creator. Exercising masculine authority on a global scale—without making oneself into the One who rules, fills, and subdues all—requires a man to lead every soul toward being a sovereign, every sovereign toward being a creator, and every creator toward being an independent, authoritative, and unique world-maker.

Section 7
A Sovereign Who Elevates Sovereigns

A masculine creator lives and dies to protect the sovereignty of each and every soul. Such a man patrols God's world with the intent to strike down the taking-tactics of everyone attempting to gain authority over anyone. While on patrol, a man will also ennoble those he sees, feels, and experiences exercising their sovereign authority without violating the sovereign authority of others. Consequently, each masculine creator obstructs world takers and ennobles world makers to preserve the orchestrational order essential for humanity, creation, and the Creator to work together in bringing forth a race of unique world makers who are making a world of unique worlds.

Chapter 19
Patrolling for Takers

Since every soul is born living spiritually independent from the World Maker, we're all world takers. Therefore, the purpose of a man patrolling God's world is not to identify who is a taker but to obstruct everyone as a taker. Despite everyone's need for a man's repulsive service, the way a man cuts down humanity's taking-tactics must be surgical. Diligently honing a mental, emotional, and physical sensitivity to everyone's nature as a taker is what allows a man to strike with a precision that leaves the material atoms unharmed while eviscerating the desire to be like God that is welling up from within each tainted soul.

The more skillful the masculine creator, the more surgically he will employ his forceful repulsion. Aggression comes naturally to a man. Most men can aggressively push back against another's body, some can aggressively push back against another's heart, and a few can aggressively push back against another's mind. However, only a masculine creator can aggressively push back another's soul without adversely affecting their mind, heart, and body.

It is pointless to spend one's time trying to identify which souls are takers since we are all born fallen. Likewise, it is equally futile to attempt to identify which thoughts, emotions, and actions are laced with corrupt world-taking intentions. As a result, a man must accept the daunting reality of expunging the taking-tactics embedded within every thought, every emotion, and every action of everyone. Once a man accepts this challenge, he'll realize—to his horror—that every thought he thinks, every emotion he feels, and every action he takes is likewise laced with the enemy's desire to rule, fill, and subdue all.

As a man is awakened to the tragedy of his reality, his mind will begin assisting him by depicting the taking-tactics rising from his tainted soul. A man's mind may display dark streams of slithering corruption spreading out from the surface of his soul, through his humanity, and into creation. Then, his heart may chip in by adding an icy sensation of death to his taking-tactics as they wriggle their way out through his sovereign domain and into Mother Nature. Lastly, a man's body may also assist him by experiencing how everything he has touched, is touching, and will touch is crumbling back into the dust.

Creation lives under the oppressive weight of everyone's world-taking intentions. Since God designed her to partner with every soul, she must materially express the spiritual likeness of everyone. As a result, our mother is desperately searching for any man who is eviscerating his own taking-tactics and can do likewise for others. However, knowing the danger inherent to a man, our mother remains justifiably fearful of the damage a masculine creator can exert upon her. Therefore, minimizing the destruction of creation's good material atoms must always remain a priority in a man's repulsive efforts.

The man who does not first see, feel, and experience the spiritual corruption slithering out from his soul, sneaking through his body, and stalking creation will remain lost in the delusion that he is the one who is Good and, therefore, the Destroyer of evil. Only when a man faces the truth that he, like the first man, is the source of all corruption will he begin to hemorrhage his fallen knowledge of good and evil. Neither is experiencing the tragedy of one's fallen reality a singular event. Hemorrhaging the fallen knowledge of good and evil is a permanent state that a masculine creator must endure until the end of the present age.

Knowing the taker's taint upon one's soul as the source of all the darkness, decay, and death spreading through creation enacts a wounded warmth upon a man that is vital for him enacting the same wounded warmth upon others. Aggressively destroying the taking-tactics slithering out from within each corrupted soul requires a masculine creator to wound others, and himself, simultaneously. After all, the only reason any human being is trying to take control of God's world and God's people is due to the failure of the first man and every successive man.

Retaining a state of wounded warmth enables a man to trace the tainted corruption of the taker's likeness in others by remaining aware of it within his own soul, mind, heart, and body. Reverse engineering the destruction everyone else is exerting upon creation is dependent upon a man ceaselessly reverse engineering his own nature as a taker. Therefore, the depth to which a man has identified his taking-tactics is the limit to which he may expose and eviscerate the same within others. A man must first see, feel, and experience his desire to rule, fill, and subdue all so he might see, feel, and experience the same in those around him.

Creation—like a man's mind, heart, and body—wants to help a masculine creator identify his corruption and the corruption rising from every tainted one. Since all fallen beings remain the same untouched spiritual voids, everyone's taking-tactics exert a similar pattern of characteristics as they move out through their inner realm and toward creation's material realm. For example, all takers create thoughts that are too glorious, emotions that are strangely vacuous, and actions that are ultimately calamitous. A grand example of this repetitive pattern regularly appears in governmental legislation. At first, a proposed piece of legislation appears fantastically noble in its stated aim to feed the hungry, create jobs, or tax the rich. However, the moment anyone actually reads the bill, it will begin to feel off, unclear, and lacking substance. Only when the legislation is implemented will everyone finally experience the calamitous results that ironically produce the exact opposite of the bill's originally stated intentions. The problem with government legislation does not reside in the bill, reading, or implementation but in the spiritual intentions of those who wrote it, read it, and implemented it.

The earlier in the creative process a masculine creator obstructs a taking-tactic, the less darkness, decay, and death creation will be obligated to express. Every exertion of spiritual intentionality requires creation to form material expressions. Although a man cannot alter a world taker's soul, he can obstruct their taking-tactics from spreading unchecked into material creation. No man can save Mother Nature since she is bound to death amidst humanity's lifeless leadership. However, any man can preserve our mother for just a little while longer to provide as many souls as possible with their chance to return to our Father.

The human mind is closest to the soul, which is spiritually lost in the taker's delusion of perfection. Therefore, each mind forms thoughts that are so glorious they appear too good to be true. Then, as the heart attempts to fill those thoughts with energetic motion, it will feel the disjointed nature between the untouched soul and the perfect thought leading to feeble, erratic, and disjointed emotions. Then, the vacuous emotions will produce incongruent actions designed to express one who thinks they are the One while simultaneously feeling like no one. Finally, creation will unite herself to those actions, accelerating the entire orchestrational effort toward ever-expanding calamity.

Anyone who believes they're destined to be the One will always create thoughts that are too glorious, emotions that are strangely vacuous, and actions that are ultimately calamitous. However, a man may intervene in this process by striking at the spiritual intent to be like God that is hidden inside every human thought, emotion, and action. Masculine repulsion pushes such corruption back through the originating inner realm and toward the soul from which it came. If done with precision, the atoms within a taker's mind, heart, and body will experience minimal damage. Once the corrupt spiritual intention is repulsed, the atoms comprising the tainted soul's thoughts, emotions, and actions will rapidly return to dust and await their next opportunity to materially express a sovereign's spiritual intentions.

The taker's spiritual desire to be the One who rules, fills, and subdues all can only hide beneath creation's anatomical goodness. As a result, every tainted one's spiritual desire to be like God is always hidden inside their glorious thoughts, vacuous emotions, and calamitous actions. The level of skill a fallen being displays in hiding their desire to be like God will prove a significant barrier to a man's repulsive efforts. Therefore, the man who is patrolling for takers will do well to request the assistance of a few skilled feminine partners.

A man's first feminine partner in eviscerating taking-tactics is creation. For example, the man who simply expects taking-tactics to be revealed before him is authoritatively requesting creation's assistance. World takers are narcissistic. It's hard to even consider how one could be vainer than aspiring to be like God. Therefore, the man who stands before a world taker—including himself—with the expectation to materially see, feel, and experience how they're trying to be like God will prove an irresistible invitation to creation to mentally, emotionally, and physically express the narcissistic nature of the taker within.

Mother Nature wants to help. Furthermore, she also wants to materially express the true nature of every spiritual being. Gazing affectionately upon her atoms with the authoritative expectation to see, feel, and experience a robust material portrayal of how each one is attempting to be like the One will always prove fruitful.

The next feminine partner eager to assist a man in exposing and obstructing takers is a woman. A woman's irresistible presence will attract the nature of the taker within everyone without effort. After all, the taker did not slither up to the man but to the woman. Although much has been made regarding how the woman was the first to succumb to the taker's temptation, the first failure was not hers. Attracting God's enemy was not the problem. Instead, the one who failed to instantly strike down God's enemy was the first to fail.

A woman embodies what every taker desires—the world of unique worlds. Moving her into the presence of others will arouse the spiritual nature of the taker within everyone to slither forth. In addition, a robust embodiment of feminine creation innately animates Mother Nature's atoms. As a result, everyone's thoughts, emotions, and actions will burst into bloom before their soul has properly vetted them. Therefore, the expressions of those around an irresistible woman will lack the polish needed to achieve effective deception. Then, as the corrupt world-taking intentions of every soul slither out into view, a man may see to the repulsive work left undone by the first man.

The more forcefully and aggressively a man strikes down a taking-tactic, the less corruption he permits into creation. At the same time, the more subtly and submissively a woman attracts taking-tactics, the greater the chance her masculine partner will have in eviscerating every vestige of humanity's desire to be like God before it reaches too far into Mother Nature. The unstoppable man who patrols creation alongside an irresistible woman will find that he does not need to root out anyone's taking-tactics. Instead, the nature of the taker within everyone will simply slither forth toward the irresistible one standing beside him.

As a masculine protector and a feminine protector stroll side-by-side through God's world of unique worlds, a woman will interact with everything and everyone to arouse all the atoms to materially express every spiritual sovereign. At the same time, the masculine creator beside her will unleash his forceful repulsions upon all, like a master duelist whipping out his blade to strike with precision before sheathing his sword so quickly that no one even notices. Every cut from a masculine creator should be so clean and precise that the wounds he inflicts upon the minds, hearts, and bodies of others close instantly. Then, the only evidence of a man's work should be the strange absence of ever-increasing world-taking tactics replaced by the inexplicable presence of ever-increasing world-making tactics.

Chapter 20
Ennobling Makers

The masculine creator who patrols the material realm by himself or alongside a robust embodiment of feminine creation will obstruct everyone's world-taking intentions before ennobling everyone's world-making intentions. All spiritual beings within the material realm naturally look to a man to ennoble them with the authority they need to rule, fill, and subdue their personal portion of Mother Nature. God gives spiritual authority to each soul. However, He gave material authority to the first man, who then promptly gave it away, compelling God to enter the material realm as the Man to reclaim the first man's position of material authority over creation. Now, any man ennobled by the Man will return to the position of the first man so he might endow material authority upon all who desire to make their world alongside his world within God's world.

Anyone seeking sovereignty over any world that is not their world will be forcefully repulsed by a man. Conversely, anyone seeking sovereignty over a portion of God's world not currently within the sovereign sphere of another world-making creator will be ennobled by a man. The male body exists to partner with God by making sure that every spiritual sovereign is free to grow into a material sovereign.

Although a man cannot create spiritual sovereigns, he can recognize those who bear the Sovereign's touch by ennobling them with an equal portion of his material authority. When the first world was created, God ennobled and enabled the first man and woman so that the man might ennoble and the woman might enable each of God's unique ones. Then, God went even further by charging the first man and woman to fruitfully multiply even more world makers. The first couple was endowed with the authority to ennoble and enable each successive world maker just as they'd been ennobled and enabled by the World Maker.

God ennobled the leadership of the first man by making him the material embodiment of the Masculine Creator. Then, God enabled the assistance of the first woman by making her the material embodiment of feminine creation. God physically touched, inwardly shaped, and spiritually breathed into the first human couple with the expectation that they would do likewise and provide Him with an ever-increasing number of independent, authoritative, and unique world makers.

Each submissive soul receives ennoblement and enablement from God in the spiritual realm. Then, each awakened sovereign may exert masculine ennoblement or feminine enablement through their respective body upon all other world makers. The body containing our soul determines whether we are most effective at imparting masculine ennoblement or feminine enablement. If no man or woman exists to perform these services for humanity, then everyone ends up wandering around waiting for their recognition and validation as a world maker.

Without an embodiment of the Father and the mother to lead humanity, our species flounders amidst its collective ignorance regarding our responsibility and desire to create our own unique world within God's world. Ever since the first man and woman abnegated their positions as material sovereigns—to take their shot at becoming the spiritual Sovereign—humanity has been left without ennoblement or enablement as world makers. When a soul does not know the World Maker and has no one to recognize them as a world maker, the only remaining option is to spend one's life taking the means to make oneself into the One who can ennoble and enable everyone.

Our orchestrational mother will only recognize a man's ennoblement when it mirrors God's ennoblement. As a result, creation is presently withholding herself from fully committing to any human world maker. The agonizing sense of what our species could have been, should have been, and would have been if only the first man had retained his material position of authority over creation remains the burning shame at the heart of every fallen man.

When a woman lifts a newborn infant toward her husband, she's expecting the child's ennoblement as an independent, authoritative, and unique world-making creator. Our orchestrational mother—and the women who embody her likeness—still look expectantly to every man to endow material authority. The unspoken tragedy of this feminine expectation is that no fallen man presently occupies the first man's position, thereby inhibiting every man from ennobling anyone.

Creating a world maker requires the entirety of the original orchestrational order. First, our Father authoritatively touches, shapes, and breathes into a soul to make a unique spiritual sovereign. Then, our mother affectionately envelopes the unique spiritual sovereign with a material body. However, a man and a woman are expected to participate as well by authoritatively ennobling and affectionately enabling the child as they progress from conception toward becoming a fully independent, authoritative, and unique world-making creator. Finally, when a fully mature sovereign attains adulthood, they'll transition from being a benefactor of the process of making world makers into a participant. Through conception, gestation, and birth, a female body is privileged to partner with creation by weaving a material body around one of God's unique ones. Then, once materially delivered, the male body is privileged to partner with the Creator by ensuring the birthed sovereign develops fully into an independent, authoritative, and unique world maker.

Amidst our present fallen age, a woman's body still partners with creation by weaving a material body around each soul. However, the lack of a unique spiritual sovereign within each soul's virgin void makes the entire process of making world makers inert. Nonetheless, the process does continue and must continue. The untouched soul woven into each material body remains an embryonic, spiritual virgin ready for the Sovereign's ennobling touch. However, there are consequences to jarring a material body with the sudden and unexpected arrival of a unique spiritual being. Understanding the process of making world makers, as well as the costs inherent to the first man's choice of independence from God, will help a man adapt his ennoblement and a woman adapt her enablement to effectively lead humanity back toward being a race of unique world makers amidst the present age of world takers.

When an infant is born, their sphere of sovereignty is so small that a man's mind may only illuminate it as a minuscule dot at the center of the child's body. However, each successive moment provides a man with an opportunity for ennoblement as he forcefully pushes the child's sovereign sphere outward. Slowly, the inexperienced world maker will respond by wielding more authority over their own mind, heart, and body as a man continues expanding the growth of their sovereign sphere. Additionally, a man may also use his repulsive nature to contract the child's sovereign sphere, should they display their insufficiency to rule, fill, and subdue their inner realm. As a child progresses into adolescence, a man will place material objects under the youth's authority and watch how they use or abuse those small portions of creation. If they use the objects to make, then a father will expand their authority. However, if they use the objects to take, then he'll contract their authority.

The foremost material aid for a masculine creator's ennobling efforts is a robust embodiment of feminine creation. Since each sovereign being exists to shape a portion of creation's anatomical splendor, observing how everyone treats a robust embodiment of feminine creation is indispensable to a man's ennobling efforts. For example, young girls tend to cling to their mothers, which, at first glance, does not appear overly problematic. However, within the young girl's body is an untouched soul of infinite emptiness that is draining the feminine splendor from her mother in the hope of animating her own non-existent spiritual being. As a result, the atoms comprising a mother's body will be depleted, causing her to have little energy for world-making with her husband, other children, and nearby world makers. Therefore, a father may choose to intervene by pushing the young girl away from her mother to spend time with friends or siblings. When the girl returns, she'll likely present her father with a story or something she made while on her journey, which is a subtle way of requesting his ennoblement for her expanding authority as a feminine world maker of interconnection.

While young girls tend to cling to their mothers, young boys tend to have the opposite issue. Amidst a misplaced desire to prove themselves as masculine world makers of independence, young males tend to spend too much time away from their feminine mother, thereby degrading their ability to gently, lovingly, and authoritatively create with creation. Therefore, a father may choose to intervene by pushing his son toward his mother to work with her on some specific task. When the boy returns, he'll likely not offer a story or a trinket from his experience to display his development. Young men intuitively sense that enjoying the presence of their feminine mother will reflect poorly upon their independence. Therefore, a father will push his son toward expressing his interactions with his mother to find the means to further ennoble the young man in preparation for—one day soon—striking out to create his own unique world with feminine creation.

When a man is seeking to ennoble adult world makers, the pull of his spouse will remain the most effective means for revealing whether he should compress or expand another's sovereign domain. When brought into the presence of an irresistible embodiment of feminine creation, sovereign souls who happened to be within an adult male body will start stumbling over their steps, their words, and their eye contact.

Inexperienced masculine creators will struggle to retain an upright, linear bearing before the inward swirling attraction of an irresistible mother. Upon seeing this, a man will impart a contracting push upon the young men to reduce their material authority and impel them to return afresh to the touch of the Authority. Only amidst a young man's ever-increasing dependence upon the Creator and a growing independence from creation may he find the resilience he needs to stand upright and unaffected before an irresistible embodiment of femininity.

Sovereign souls housed within an adult female body will also reveal their level of maturity before an irresistible mother. Since each woman is a holistic embodiment of creation's universal whole, any woman of lesser allure will naturally be drawn toward, lean against, or even move in circles around the strongest epicenter of orbital attraction. These reactions reveal young women who do not yet understand their charge is to be a unique embodiment of feminine creation and not the embodiment of feminine creation. Their submissive display before an irresistible mother is in the hope that they'll receive her blessing, surpass her irresistible nature, and elevate themselves into the one who might attract the Masculine One. As a result, a masculine creator will forcefully contract the sovereign sphere of such young women to push them back from pursuing the delusion of being the most desirable one and toward being a uniquely desirable one.

As a man and a woman, a creator and creation, and a father and a mother, a couple works together to ennoble and enable everyone toward creating their own unique world within God's world. A man's touch ennobles, and a woman's touch enables everyone as a sovereign world maker. Masculine ennoblement expands or contracts the authority of each soul, while feminine enablement pulls creation's atoms toward or away from the authority of each soul. As a result, everyone who desires to be a unique world-making creator naturally seeks out a father and a mother. A father pushes everyone into a position of authority over creation, and a mother pulls creation's atoms into a position of submission under each creator so all might go forth as a race of world makers to make a world of unique worlds.

Chapter 21
Enforcing Orchestrational Order

Creation is awaiting a father's ennoblement and a mother's enablement of all human world makers. God made the first man and woman as the sovereigns of His world. Consequently, creation still honors the Creator's original design. Furthermore, both the Creator and creation are restraining themselves from interfering in the present fallen age out of respect for the original orchestrational order. Therefore, a man and a woman are still expected to represent and lead humanity in the original world-making partnership between the Creator, creation, and every human creator.

Although humanity has rejected the original orchestrational order, the Creator and creation have remained loyal. Ironically, we condemn our Father and our mother for not intervening on our behalf when their restraint from interfering with fallen humanity has preserved the faint and fleeting opportunity for each of us to reclaim our original position at the epicenter of orchestration. Therefore, as a couple returns to representing humanity, they'll be expected to resume the ennoblement and enablement of world makers before the Creator and creation while enforcing orchestrational order between every member of our species.

Once creation recognizes a man's ennoblement and a woman's enablement of a growing world-maker, she'll obediently open herself to the unique one. Our mother wants to know and uniquely express anyone uplifted by a man and a woman as a sovereign. As created beings, we do not recognize our own authority. God recognized the first two authorities so they might recognize each successive authority. Even amidst the presently cursed, corrupted, and condemned age, our mother still yearns to obediently open herself, submit to, and worship each one

175

touched by the Unique One. However, she'll only do so if the original orchestrational order is honored. Any world maker not ennobled by one representing the Father and not enabled by one representing the mother will not receive creation's wholehearted, submissive obedience.

A man's ennoblement lifts a creator up before creation so she may submissively serve them as if they were him. We know this because that is how God originally endowed the first man with His authority to rule, fill, and subdue His world. Conversely, a woman pulls creation's atoms toward each soul so that Mother Nature might submissively serve each sovereign in a manner reminiscent of how her body submissively serves her husband and her soul submissively serves God. Then, each ennobled and enabled world maker may authoritatively uplift their portion of submissive material creation to lead Mother Nature toward bringing forth their unique world so she might continue growing toward becoming God's world of unique worlds.

Despite the inevitability of conflict between human world makers, our combative interactions flow from the original design intended to engender a world of unique worlds. Wherever two sovereign spheres touch, a temporary point of interconnection is formed between both worlds that brings both sovereigns running to defend their domain. However, if a father and a mother are present to enforce orchestrational order, the unfolding situation may be led away from a conflict between two world takers and back toward a conversation between two world makers.

Defusing the conflict between two sovereigns is best achieved when a father first moves in between both combatants to push them apart before a mother follows to pull them back together. As a man steps forward, he must immediately strike down the taking-tactics initially being unleashed by each sovereign. Inexperienced world makers will remain largely unaware that all their thoughts, emotions, and actions are saturated with world-taking intentionality. Each sovereign's attempt to protect their world is actually a complex strategy designed to take their opponent's world, feeding an ever-increasing cycle of taking until both know nothing but destruction. Therefore, a father leads by stepping in between both sovereigns so he might unleash a series of successive strikes to diffuse each combatant's initial onslaught of taking-tactics.

Allegorizing the inner realm will help a man recognize how to repulse the taking-tactics of each soul while minimizing the damage to their minds, hearts, and bodies. Our inner realm is actually a living garden where our soul is the gardener, our thoughts are the seeds we sow, our emotions are the trees we grow, and our actions are the fruit we harvest. When a masculine creator strikes down the world-taking intentions of another, he must wield his repulsive force like an elegant rapier to pierce the fruit of action being harvested by a body. Then, while momentarily holding the fruit of action in place, a man will thrust his repulsive blade back through the emotional tree that grew the action to puncture the mental seed that spawned its growth. Once a man has completely skewered the taking action back through the taking emotion and into the taking thought, he may then lunge to push the spiritual intent to take out of the action, emotion, and thought and back into the soul from which it came.

Executing a forceful strike of repulsion backward through the entirety of another soul's creative process—with minimal damage to the atoms comprising their mind, heart, or body—is a refined skill. However, a masculine creator intent on enforcing orchestrational order must be able to unleash such strikes in rapid succession and with lightning precision. Ideally, every repulsive blow should be so swift that no one even realizes what is happening. Then, the momentary pause that a father's strikes procure—as each combatant's thoughts, emotions, and actions crumble back into the dust amidst the abrupt removal of their spiritual intentions—is when a man will usher his alluring partner in between both combatants.

Before addressing a mother's role in enforcing orchestrational order between combative sovereigns, it's important to note that a man should avoid publicly exposing anyone's corrupt spiritual intentions, perverse thoughts, deceptive emotions, or pathetic actions. Usually, having a combatant know that you know is enough. The masculine creator who finds himself tempted to reveal what he knows still desires to elevate himself over others. Only when a combatant grows belligerent toward a father's intervention should a man consider exerting more aggressive forms of revelation to hold the combatant in place in preparation for a mother's touch. A man exists to uplift humanity. Any effort to publicly disgrace another human being is counterproductive to the charge laid upon the first man, reclaimed by the Man, and now exerted by any resurrected man.

Once a man has expertly cut down the initial taking-tactics of both combative sovereigns, he'll then step aside and let his feminine partner move onto the point where both sovereign's spheres are touching. First, by merely positioning herself at the point of conflict, a mother allows both combatants to see what they're fighting over. Fallen beings do not recognize creation as a living and active partner. She is a thing that we use, misuse, and abuse without consequence. However, seeing an irresistible embodiment of Mother Nature standing precisely at the confluence of atoms being fought over induces a poignant revelation of shame for all involved in a conflict.

After a woman's irresistible presence reminds both combatants of the feminine partner they're fighting over, she'll then pull each toward herself amidst her genuine desire to form a mutually beneficial partnership of independently interconnected interdependence. At the same time, a father will continue to strike down any taking-tactics he senses taking shape from within either sovereign. Then, a mother may safely expand her alluring nature with understanding smiles, affectionate touches, and soothing words to plant her mother's seed into the minds, hearts, and bodies of both combatants. Like creation, a woman wants to permanently affix the point of interconnection between both world makers' worlds, so they'll continue growing together amidst her world of unique worlds.

As a mother's seed takes root, her effervescent presence will accelerate its germination. Then, both combative sovereigns will start to see, feel, and experience how vital the other might soon become to their own world-making effort. A mother's seed lets each sovereign perceive their world as the centerpiece of her world of unique worlds, helping each to recognize how vital their world might soon become to their fellow sovereign and vice versa. However, like creation, a woman will not tell the combatants how to form a functional partnership as independent, interconnected, and interdependent world-making creators. Instead, she'll merely expect them to figure that out on their own amidst their earnest desire to remain in good standing with her as their embodiment of our orchestrational mother.

A woman's greatest leverage in enforcing orchestrational order is to subtly infer that maintaining her as a partner requires maintaining a partnership with everyone. After all, the world of unique worlds does not make any allowance for dissension. Being a uniquely irresistible feminine partner and a limitless source of orchestrational potential is a woman's most effective means for ensuring orchestrational order between every world and every world maker within her world of unique worlds.

Creation's principal purpose is a world of unique worlds. The woman who enforces orchestrational order to ensure that end will make herself indispensable to creation. At the same time, the Creator's principal purpose is a race of unique world makers. The man who enforces orchestrational order to ensure that end will make himself indispensable to the Creator. Therefore, a couple enforces orchestrational order by pushing and pulling everyone back into the arms of our spiritual Father and our material mother so that each unique world maker might see to the orchestration of the most important and indispensable world amidst God's world of unique worlds.

Section 8
A Creator Who Creates Creators

God made the first world and the first man with the expectation
that each man would make his own world to make world makers.
Unfortunately, once the first man abdicated his position of material
authority, every subsequent man was left adrift and helpless before the
coursing currents of anatomical creation. However, now that God has
claimed a male body for Himself, the opportunity is open for any man to
return to the Man so he might reclaim the first man's position as a
divergent epicenter of material authority. Therefore, any masculine
creator who submits to the Man may return to leading each authoritative
body toward material orchestration as God leads each submissive soul
toward spiritual manifestation.

Chapter 22
The Currents of Creation

Every micro and macro element of creation displays our mother's irresistible orbital allure. The feminine motion of each atom is mirrored by each solar system, each galaxy, and ultimately the entire universe. Creation maintains her inward pulling displays to ensure that no one forgets how she orbits around, looks to, and lives for only the One. Additionally, any soul caught amidst her coursing anatomical currents will find themselves regularly and repetitiously disabused of the delusion that they are the One. No matter how hard an untouched soul might thrash for recognition amidst creation's currents, they'll remain irrelevant and swept along amidst her realm of time, space, and matter. However, what we fear most is when the currents of creation pull our soul under and spit us out to permanently affix our present spiritual state of being nothing, nowhere, and no one for all eternity.

Children conceptualize creation as landscapes, plants, and animals. However, she's far more. Creation is also the air we breathe, the vacuous expanse of the heavens above, and all the mysteries we have shamefully failed to explore throughout her wondrous universal whole. The only object in anatomical creation that is not permanently a part of Mother Nature is our spiritual soul. Recognizing one's irrelevance to and helplessness before our mother's tumultuous expanse of femininity is where every man starts and where every man ultimately ends. Any man who attempts to reclaim the first man's authority so he might lead humanity back into the original orchestrational partnership must experience the full scope of his utter insignificance before the universal expanse of our orchestrational mother.

We study creation and the alluring ways she moves only to conclude again and again that we do not understand, we do not control, and we do not have any say in how she carries us along. The moment we claim to know her is the moment she is eagerly awaiting to expand our ignorance. In the same way that young men despair when a beautiful woman looks straight through them as if they do not exist, so creation looks straight through every untouched soul because we do not exist.

As creation's anatomical currents ebb and flow around us, small portions of her material nature do get briefly caught up in the eddy-like depression caused by our lightless, loveless, and lifeless souls. However, her atoms only linger to fulfill the Creator's desire that each spiritual being receives the means for material expression. After experiencing humanity's unaltered state of spiritual nonexistence for millennia, our orchestrational mother is slowly coming to the tragic conclusion that no unique ones exist who are capable of authoritatively leading her toward becoming God's world of unique worlds.

We do not understand our mother because we do not understand our Father. Creation moves in such confounding ways because those patterns were first inspired by her Creator. Even more importantly, all our mother's original movements—that were designed to enable everyone's world-making efforts—have been cursed by God to obstruct everyone's world-taking efforts. Still, our mother has not fully given up her hope in finding unique ones. Her coursing currents are still searching amidst the fading dream that she might somehow find those capable of leading her toward pleasing her Beloved.

In the ways that creation used to desire to help us, she now desires to hurt us. Our mother's anatomical currents have swollen into a raging sea, desperately searching for any being of spiritual existence to vent her frustration upon. Those awakened by God's touch amidst the present fallen age will receive a greeting from creation far different than what they would've experienced prior to the failure of the first man.

Being a vacuous soul of untouched spiritual emptiness is not our problem. Mother Nature began her existence as a void, and she's intrinsically drawn to anyone who shares the same origin. The problem is when creation cannot see, feel, or experience her Beloved's touch upon our soul's void. Our mother cannot comprehend why anyone would avoid God's touch. As a result, the minuscule sphere of sovereignty she maintains around each soul is merely due to her obligation to ensure that she does not miss a unique one rising unexpectedly from within our void.

The more a man embraces his utter insignificance before Mother Nature, the more rapidly he'll rise into a self-defining, co-defining, and global-defining authority. Only by seeing, feeling, and experiencing one's helplessness before the universal feminine sea will a man know his ceaseless desperation for the Masculine One. Additionally, a man's personal revelation of his irrelevance amidst creation cannot be an isolated event. A man must live in a perpetual state of terror amidst creation's currents to remain forever conscious of what will happen the moment he removes his soul from God's touch. Only while anchored to God in the spiritual realm may a man stand upright amidst creation's currents to endure her righteous fury and authoritatively lead her back toward humanity so all might make her into our world of unique worlds.

A man must ceaselessly develop an awareness of his insignificance before our mother so he might know exactly why he must remain dependent upon our Father. Attempting to authoritatively orchestrate even a small portion of creation's atoms away from the forms originally established by the Creator is the personification of insolence. Still, this is the exact level of authority that God desires each man to wield. Failing to seize the position thrown away by the first man, reclaimed by the Man, and now open to any man is an insult to our Father's sacrifice and our mother's hope.

In the beginning, the One who is Something, Somewhere, and Someone touched, shaped, and breathed a material and spiritual authority into existence. Since that day, the cyclical currents of creation have been searching for the unique ones promised to arrive through the first man. Today, creation is still waiting, albeit in a frighteningly agitated state. Any man who honors our mother's faithful expectation by returning his soul to God will not receive any acclaim for his valiant choice. Instead, creation's coursing currents will pull his soul into the depths of her rage to crush him beneath the full weight of every man's failure—since the fall of the first man—for which she'll hold him solely responsible.

Mother is tired of dealing with our mess while having no man willing to take responsibility for humanity. Anyone who attempts to stand before her will receive all she's been storing up since the first man unwittingly abandoned her to the taker's clutches. Creation will now treat any man who aspires to lead humanity harshly, unfairly, and mercilessly. Nonetheless, enduring the caustic currents of creation is the duty of a doomed man. The unbearable burden to lead our species toward world-making amidst all the consequences engendered by our world-taking will fall squarely upon the shoulders of any man who stands before our enraged orchestrational mother.

With each passing generation, creation has grown more bitter in her fruitless search to find independent, authoritative, and unique world makers. Our mother is angry. However, it's not for the reason we think. Creation is angry because she dreads displeasing her Beloved. Tragically, we're creation's only means to please her Creator. Without us, she cannot become God's world of unique worlds, perpetually producing unique world makers. Our mother is not specifically angry at us for what we've done. Rather, she's angry at us for who we've failed to become.

Amidst our mother's growing desperation, she is clinging to each lifeless soul far longer than she should. Unfortunately, the longer she clings to a void of infinite emptiness, the more our souls drain away the effervescence of her atoms. When she is eventually forced to release an untouched soul, Mother Nature both gasps with sorrow and sighs with relief. The compounding effect of holding so many untouched souls for so long has created an unalterable trajectory in her atoms, leading her inexorably toward ever-increasing darkness, decay, and, ultimately, death.

The moment a man's soul is touched by God, he'll spiritually awaken amidst a material realm that is dying because of him. Should he attempt to lead our mother back toward humanity, he'll find the caustic currents of creation turning against him. Our material mother will ceaselessly strive to drown each masculine creator with the ever-increasing darkness, decay, and death that all humanity is obligating her to express. Amidst her present state, creation will show no mercy. Our mother knows that the greatest assistance she may provide a man is to make his life debt unbearable. Creation has learned from experience that if she relents for even a moment, the faint forms of light, love, and life, which are only faintly flickering in one who has only recently known her Creator's touch, will wink out. Therefore, our orchestrational mother will ensure each awakened masculine creator knows only ever-increasing toil, suffering, and failure all his days so that he might tremble in fear at what she'll do to him the moment he withdraws his soul from the touch of her Beloved.

Every man bearing the spiritual lineage of the first man is the problem. Worse yet, the best thing a man's leadership can offer creation is an extension of her agonizing labor. When a man pushes back the corruption spreading from each untouched soul, he only lengthens the agony our mother is experiencing along her unalterable trajectory toward death. Additionally, a man's arrival as a unique spiritual being will also confirm creation's deepest fear—that, for millennia, she has not been pleasing her Beloved by bringing forth His race of unique world makers so she might become His world of unique worlds.

Mother lives to please Father. The arrival of a unique one intent on leading humanity back into the original world-making partnership will only confirm to creation how upset her Creator is with humanity and possibly her. Being one who validates our mother's greatest fear is not an enviable position. Still, with no solution to offer, a man merely accepts holistic responsibility for humanity so he may do what the first man failed to do, what the Man came to do, and what he now wants to do.

A man cannot offer creation a solution. Instead, a man can only extend creation's suffering by leading her to continue to carry as many untouched souls as possible so each might have their opportunity to return to their Creator. The man who holds our mother back from death by extending the duration of her suffering will only engender ever-increasing hatred from the first feminine partner. However, a masculine creator exists to serve the wishes of our Father, not our mother. Leading creation to materially sustain as many untouched souls as possible so more might spiritually return to God is a torture that a masculine creator will not be able to comprehend but will still not hesitate to inflict.

The Man leads humanity and creation. However, the Man decided to withdraw His leadership from the material realm until all submissive souls have been gathered. Only then will He remake the entire material universe in preparation for eternally restoring the original world-making partnership. The Man has already accepted the full consequences of what His people are producing. Any man who chooses to do likewise must suffer as the Man suffered by reclaiming the position of material authority over our enraged orchestrational mother to lead her back into the broken partnership with human creators and the Creator.

God's principal purpose remains unchanged. He still desires to make independent, authoritative, and unique world makers above all else. Furthermore, He's also concluded that the present circumstances we've created amidst our cursed, corrupted, and condemned age have brought forth an ideal environment from which to discover which souls are dedicated, defiant, and determined enough to pursue Him, despite the consequences. The Man's apparent abandonment of humanity amidst the present age is confusing to some. However, the One who is Authority is far more interested in making authorities than He is in exerting authority.

When a man arises from God's touch to stand before the raging storm of creation's caustic currents, he reclaims the first man's task to represent humanity at the epicenter of the original world-making partnership. Someone must take the brunt of the torrential onslaught our species has engendered from our embittered orchestrational mother. The Man has shown us how incomprehensible the cost is for any man who returns to live as a masculine creator. Additionally, should a man striving to lead humanity falter, then creation's unrelenting currents will sweep him away, along with everyone braced against him as their bulwark amidst our mother's unquenchable rage.

As a man struggles to stand erect before creation's coursing currents, he'll find that there is one who might help him. However, the Creator will not assist a man in his material struggles because, as the Father, He does not wish to deprive any of His sons of the resistance vital for developing mental dedication, emotional defiance, and physical determination. Similarly, creation will not abate her rage simply to allow a representative of fallen humanity to have an easier time. However, it is possible that a woman may take it upon herself to assist a man who is standing alone before the caustic currents of creation.

A man is ill-suited to stand before Mother Nature precisely because he embodies the failure of the first man. A woman, on the other hand, is a different story. The one who embodies the entirety of feminine creation may speak to our mother on behalf of her man and humanity. A woman wants what creation wants—a world of unique worlds. However, she'll not ask creation to abate her righteous rage simply to spare her husband and humanity. Instead, a woman will commune with Mother Nature to convince her that hope still remains to please her Beloved by laboring on in bringing forth more world makers. Although amidst the present age of death and dust, becoming a world of unique worlds is technically a lost cause for creation, a woman may convince creation that she is still pleasing God by bearing as many world makers as possible and preparing them as much as possible for the age of creators yet to come.

Like an aging wife who has systematically traced all her sorrows back to her husband, creation is slowly tracing all her sorrows back to the first man and each of his masculine descendants. Still, as a man struggles to push back against the caustic currents of creation, a woman may help by pulling her husband, and all those sheltering behind him into the eye of the storm between the arms of the Creator and creation to engender something like the original world-making partnership. Achieving such an outcome requires a woman to negotiate as humanity's representative before Mother Nature while her husband strains to shelter our species from creation's fury. Then, a woman may begin authoritatively pulling creation's atoms to obey her—as if she is the orchestrational mother—to lead a vast portion of the material realm back toward becoming a world of unique worlds.

The present goal of a man and a woman is not to undo what has been done, is being done, and will continue to be done by humanity to our orchestrational mother. Creation's fate has already been sealed by our species. Now, the only goal remaining is to buy humanity as much time as possible amidst the caustic currents of creation so that as many souls as possible might return to the original world-making partnership.

Chapter 23
Epicenters of Authority

As a fallen species, our untouched souls each form a perforation in creation, draining her finite orchestrational capacity into each of our infinitely empty voids. The longer we linger within our material bodies, the more we take from creation in a doomed attempt to make ourselves into the Creator. The only solution to our perforation in creation is to plug it with a living epicenter of world-making authority empowered by God to pour forth unique expressions of light, love, and life.

The moment God's touch impregnates our virgin, embryonic soul, a spiritual being is born who will invert the present process of draining Mother Nature. Once anyone exists as a unique one, they'll begin overflowing with their own unique expressions of luminous light, flowing love, and fiery life. Although a resurrected being will invert the effect they're personally exerting upon creation, the plugging of one spiritual perforation is meaningless to the total effect humanity is exerting upon our mother. Still, a unique one does become a surging well of mental light, emotional love, and physical life that will infuse creation's fading currents and temporarily produce a unique world that will briefly arouse our mother's desire to continue as God's world of unique worlds.

Untouched souls are draining creation as they're helplessly carried along by her currents. Touched souls stand unmoved within creation's currents as a divergent epicenter of authority within God's world. Being anchored to God amidst a timeless, spaceless, and matterless spiritual union is what enables a unique one to stand as their own divergent epicenter of authority amidst creation's fuming atoms. However, the mental illuminations, emotional currents, and fiery actions we pour forth into creation will only rejuvenate the atoms within our sovereign sphere.

Additionally, since all creation's atoms are transient, any enduring effects a single living sovereign might engender will be negated amidst the billions of untouched souls currently draining the natural world. Nonetheless, the luminous light of our mind, the flowing love of our heart, and the fiery life of our body mark us as an epicenter of authority that will inspire creation to labor on in her doomed union with humanity.

Existing as a spiritual epicenter of authority inverts the human experience. Untouched souls cling to creation, desperate to remain within her affectionate material embrace. Conversely, creation clings to each soul touched by God amidst her desperation to keep us within her affectionate material embrace. As the originally intended connection between the Creator and creation, each human being is a conduit designed to conduct the Creator's love to creation and her reciprocations. Our mother looks expectantly toward us to keep her connected to our Father. She aches for the opportunity to display her love toward her Creator through her submissive obedience toward us. Therefore, the more we frantically burrow into the Creator's spiritual embrace, the more creation will frantically envelop us in her material embrace.

As fallen beings, we've grown quite accomplished at manipulating creation's desire for her Creator. We intuitively sense that she needs us. Therefore, we leverage that to demand that she submit unconditionally to us. In exchange, we promise Mother Nature that we'll grant her an audience with God—the moment we become God. However, our mother is starting to figure out that if she helps us become like God, then we'd replace her Beloved, destroy her, and remake everything and everyone into our likeness.

The moment a perforation within creation is plugged with a living epicenter of orchestrational authority, the original world-making partnership between the Creator, creation, and human creators is reformed, albeit on a micro-scale. Each mental illumination, emotional current, and fiery action we bring forth is akin to a flare fired into the air, signaling the existence of a unique one. Contrasted against the withering splendor of our orchestrational mother, the specter of a unique epicenter of authority spewing forth never-before-seen light, water, and fire is a jarring spectacle.

Unfortunately, random explosions of uniqueness will not satiate our mother's desire for orderly orchestration. She expects ever-increasing imagery, auras, and styles of actions that honor the Masculine Creator and her as His feminine creation. She also expects our unique forms of mental light, emotional currents, and fiery actions to remain centered upon the two bodies that she's worked so diligently to perpetuate on our behalf. She further expects each united man and woman to lead every soul back toward her Creator so our entire species might finally begin reconnecting her to the touch of her Beloved.

Once the Creator's touch plugs the infinite drain within a man's soul with a new spiritual being of world-making authority, then he may present himself as a biological, surrogate, or symbolic father to other aspiring world makers. However, a man will not push creation to submit to anyone. Instead, he'll push everyone toward the Unique One so they might be someone creation will submit to on her own accord.

Every human mind, heart, and body is born without a spiritual sovereign within their soul. As a result, everyone's inner realm has grown accustomed to looking outward for leadership. A man may intentionally disrupt this habit by presenting himself as the foremost external authority. Then, instead of compelling the mind, heart, and body of another to obey him, he'll compel that mind, heart, and body to obey their spiritual sovereign, who is rising from within their soul from the Sovereign's inseminating touch.

A man's ability to exert masculine repulsion at least one magnitude beyond what any other external source can muster is what allows him to arrest the wayward tendencies of every mind, heart, and body. However, a man does not discipline anyone's mind, heart, and body for failing to obey their rightful sovereign. Instead, he disciplines each soul by revealing how their mind, heart, and body do not even recognize them as a sovereign. Then, as a world maker rises from God's touch, a man may assist the newly risen being by pushing their mind, heart, and body back from submitting to any external authorities so their inner realm will have no choice but to submit to their rightful authority.

If there is a woman alongside a man, she may likewise offer herself as a biological, surrogate, or symbolic mother to enable every nearby world maker. As a unique embodiment of creation, a woman is capable of illuminating, animating, and regenerating the atoms comprising any sovereign's sphere to increase how rapidly their world will rise. The stronger the attraction a woman's spiritual being emanates, the more she may impart that attraction to the atoms and strengthen the bond between any spiritual world maker and their personal portion of Mother Nature. A woman's leadership is most effective not by invigorating each spiritual creator to unite with material creation but by invigorating material creation to unite with each spiritual creator.

A mother leads humanity and creation by pulling each unique world toward serving every other unique world. Immature worlds will benefit greatly as a mother subtly exposes them to other, more mature worlds. Since a mature sovereign should not be forming a partnership with an inexperienced world maker, a mother's seed planted inside a young world ensures that it will grow toward serving all worlds. The mother who subtly implants the world-making intentions of all world makers inside every world is leading every world toward a deeper interconnection within God's world of unique worlds.

As young world makers receive a father's ennoblement and a mother's enablement, they'll begin touching, shaping, and breathing their unique likeness into the submissive atoms within their sovereign sphere. Then, the pale and drained anatomical expanse of Mother Nature will start erupting with more epicenters of illuminating light, flowing love, and living fire. As the effects of the unique ones spread throughout creation, a father and a mother will stroll among the developing authorities to enforce orchestrational order as all begin interacting amidst God's world.

Young epicenters of authority will look to a father and a mother for guidance regarding how far they might push or pull creation toward becoming their unique world. However, creation's innate flexibility is not limited by how far we push or pull her but by how much illicit world-taking intentionality remains hidden inside our push or pull. Inexperienced creators cannot separate their world-making tactics from their world-taking tactics. They'll have a hard time sensing how every outward-pushing aggression and inward-pulling attraction is aimed at taking every world so that they might become the One who is ruling, filling, and subduing the entirety of God's world. Therefore, a father will need to remain close to push back everyone's world-taking intentions while a mother remains close to pull out everyone's world-making intentions.

The couple who co-creates together within one shared inner realm is preparing themselves to lead all humanity toward co-creating together within one shared material realm. A man pushes everyone toward being an independent epicenter of authority to fulfill our Father's desire for a race of unique world makers. At the same time, a mother pulls everyone's world toward their epicenter of authority to fulfill our mother's desire for a world of unique worlds. Together, a man pushes humanity back into the arms of the Creator as a woman pulls humanity back into the arms of creation so each epicenter of authority might erupt with ever-increasing luminescent light, flowing love, and living fire.

Chapter 24
Manifestation Before Orchestration

As fallen beings, we all have an insatiable yearning for instantaneous, magical manifestation. Our obsession with figuring out how to summon forth something from nothing comes from our inability to summon forth someone from the nothingness within our soul. Still, we do find hope in draining material creation for the means to attain our spiritual manifestation. The tactic we still employ today is the same tactic the first man and woman originally employed when reaching for the forbidden fruit. The first-time humanity consumed material creation to enable our spiritual manifestation failed. However, we still persist in the same strategy amidst the delusional hope that the next material object we consume will finally be the one that manifests us into the Unique One. Each tainted soul remains committed to the original taking tactic because the only alternative is to surrender our spiritual independence from God by acknowledging that all our efforts without Him, to become like Him, have failed.

The taker's temptation to consume what God materially orchestrated to enable our spiritual manifestation was, is, and always will remain absurd. A material object bound within creation's finite realm of time, space, and matter simply cannot manifest a perfect replication of Infinite Fullness from a soul of infinite emptiness. Still, the first man and woman heartily embraced the taker's temptation, not because of its sound logic but because it offered us something God never would.

The Creator never offered us the opportunity to be like Him. Even if God did want to offer us the opportunity, He could not, for He is the One who is unlike anyone. The offer God did make, and still makes to humanity, is to receive and grow into our own likeness of His uniqueness, which—over time—will make everyone more and more unlike anyone, including, unlike God.

Picturing a pyramid offers a simple way to conceptualize the difference between being like God and bearing God's likeness. When the taker tempted the first man and woman, he suggested that they were at the bottom of the pyramid while God sat alone at the hierarchical pinnacle of Perfection. After painting such a galling depiction of inferiority, all the taker then had to do was point toward the one thing that gave humanity the hope of an instantaneous ascension to the pinnacle of Perfection. And clearly, the only material thing that promised the possibility of magical manifestation was the one thing God forbade humanity from consuming amidst the whole of Mother Nature.

Reorienting oneself away from the original taking-tactic requires merely flipping the pyramid on its head. Once the pyramid is upside down, we may see how each soul begins at the exact same point of unchanging, lifeless perfection as a void of infinite spiritual emptiness. Then, as we're collectively touched by the Unique One, everyone erupts upward and outward along their own trajectory of uniqueness. With each passing moment, we grow more and more unlike one another. The upside-down pyramid reveals God's intent for everyone He touches to grow upward and outward into their own likeness of His uniqueness.

A fallen being's opportunity to orchestrate within creation ends the moment they claim to have attained the pinnacle of Perfection. The instant anyone exalts in having finally attained equality with God is the moment all creation and every human creator recoil in horror. As a result, every world and every world maker who'd previously been helping an untouched soul achieve their hierarchical aspiration will withdraw their support, leaving the lightless, loveless, and lifeless soul alone atop their imploding world. When reflecting upon these narcissistic moments, we can see each moment of pride that preceded each fall. However, these moments also reveal how incapable an untouched soul is at upholding anything. Like the fallen one, fallen beings need to deceive creation and human creators to build a world for them that allows them to look, feel, and act like God. However, the moment we sit atop our pinnacle of Perfection—with the intent to rule, fill, and subdue like God—then all our deceptive schemes are revealed, all our partners leave, and we're left alone atop an imploding world.

Once God's touch magically manifests a unique spiritual being from within our soul of infinite emptiness, we flip the taker's pyramid of Perfection upside down. No longer do we need to waste our life climbing any form of hierarchy. The moment God touches our submissive soul, we're already ascending upward and outward along our own trajectory into a never-before-seen spiritual likeness that cannot be compared, contrasted, or competed against. Then, our mind, heart, and body will excitedly begin expressing our growing uniqueness, for which there is no end.

God alone manifests someone from nothing. Then, we materially orchestrate creation's atoms into a unique world that will express the unique one that God has already spiritually manifested. The present moment is the only moment for God's manifesting work upon our soul, causing creation's atoms around us to ripple with the delayed effects of material orchestration. Consequently, timeless spiritual manifestation is what impels all time-based material orchestration.

A man pushes himself, creation, and humanity back toward the Father to lead all toward the means for spiritual manifestation. At the same time, a woman pulls herself, the Creator, and humanity back toward our mother to lead all toward the means for material orchestration. Therefore, a couple who is pushing everyone toward the Creator for spiritual manifestation while also pulling everyone toward creation for material orchestration is reforming the original world-making partnership in preparation for producing an ever-increasing number of independent, authoritative, and unique world makers who will work together to make Mother Nature into our world of their unique worlds.

Section 9
A Maker Who Makes World Makers

A masculine creator designs his world as an ideal material environment for maturing spiritual sovereigns into independent, authoritative, and unique world-makers. First, God must spiritually elevate a man's soul into an independent master so a man might materially lead his mind, heart, and body to do the same. Then, as one who is growing less and less dependent upon anything or anyone—other than the One—a man may lead his marriage toward becoming humanity's epicenter of interconnecting love by using his body to conduct the Creator's love out into creation while his wife uses her body to conduct creation's love back toward the Creator. Finally, as a man matures into a global-defining authority, he'll willfully expend the remainder of his days making unique world makers so he might partner with the most mentally profound, emotionally potent, and physically powerful sovereigns of his age.

Chapter 25
An Independent Master of Ascension

Independent mastery is unattainable in the material realm due to every atom of Mother Nature remaining permanently interconnected within her splendid, universal whole. Still, creation allows us to temporarily reorchestrate our personal portion of her atoms so we might express ourselves as one being touched by the Independent Master. What creation will not allow is for even one of her atoms to be permanently removed from her submissive service to the Independent Master. As a result, the only place we attain independent mastery is in the spiritual realm, where we must remain wholly dependent upon God. Therefore, independent mastery is never something a created being fully attains but something we have the privilege of perpetually growing toward through our spiritual union with our Creator. Only when a man bows before the Independent Master will he begin growing into an independent master capable of elevating his inner realm, his personal portion of creation's material realm, and any world makers who look to him for leadership.

God independently mastered creation by making her into His world of unique worlds for the purpose of growing His race of unique world makers. As a result, we submit our soul to God that so He might make us into the unique ones He desires. Then, as a growing and independent world maker, we may go forth to authoritatively lead our personal portion of God's dependent world toward becoming our independent world.

There is only one Independent Master. However, anyone touched by Him will be uplifted into ever-increasing independent mastery. Still, God's work upon our soul never ends with us attaining full mastery or independence. As a spiritual being, our potential for growth is limitless, as long as we don't fall for deception that there is an end. The end for a fallen being is to be like God while the end for a resurrected being is the next touch from the One who is their Beginning and their End.

God did not make human beings so that we might merely submit. Our Creator already has a vast host to worship and serve Him. What God wants from humanity is a race of independent, authoritative, and unique world-makers. The Master requires our spiritual submission so He might uplift us into our own likeness of His independent mastery. Then, we're free to do likewise by uplifting our personal portion of dependent creation toward becoming our independent world.

Untouched souls cannot uplift anything. Their only desire is to force everything and everyone to submit until all exist as something less than their lightless, loveless, and lifeless souls. Then, once an untouched soul forces everything and everyone downward beneath their non-existent spiritual likeness, an untouched soul will climb the pile of corpses they've created to take themselves to their pinnacle of Perfection.

Without spiritual ascension, any demand for material submission can only lead to darkness, decay, and death. God alone is the Independent Master because He alone exists in the ascended position of Uniqueness. Our Creator is the only One capable of making everyone into their own never-before-seen likeness of His uniqueness because He is only the One who has always been, and will always be, Unique.

God elevates each submissive soul into a growing independent master so we might join Him in the original world-making partnership. Fallen beings waste their lives trying to make themselves like God so they might take God's position in the original world-making partnership. Unfortunately for fallen beings, God's position as the Independent Master of Ascension is not an elected position. God is in that position because He is the only One capable of uplifting everyone into their own never-before-seen likeness of His uniqueness.

The ascension of our soul is an instantaneous event of spiritual manifestation that only takes place in the present moment of timeless faith. Furthermore, the touch conceiving, sustaining, and growing our unique spiritual being exerts a persistent effect that is utterly separate from material time, space, and matter. Our faith-based, spiritual submission in the present moment is what allows each believer to know that God has already made them—and is continuing to make them—into their own likeness of His uniqueness. Consequently, any attempt to use any form of time, space, and matter to elevate oneself utterly eliminates our opportunity to receive the present-moment touch of the Independent Master, thereby condemning our soul to remain an untouched, formless void.

Within the original orchestrational partnership, the first two positions are filled and non-negotiable. The first position goes to God because He is the only One capable of spiritually ennobling everyone. The second position goes to creation because she is the one designed by God to materially enable everyone. Only after we've embraced the first two members of the original orchestrational partnership as irreplaceable will it then become apparent that it falls to us to create our own irreplaceable position within the original orchestrational partnership.

The Creator and creation do not offer any fixed positions within their world-making partnership. Each unique one is responsible for making their own irreplaceable position. A sovereign soul bearing their own likeness of Uniqueness takes it upon themselves to make themselves uniquely valuable to the Creator, creation, and every human creator.

The positions of the Creator and creation within the original world-making partnership are fixed. However, our position is not. Our Father ennobles us as independent, authoritative, and unique world makers and our mother enables us with her atoms so that we might make our own unique world within her as God's world of unique worlds. Still, we must make our world in a way that positions us as valuable members of the original world-making partnership. As the fall of mankind proves, human beings are free to do whatever they want. However, forming a partnership requires that we do whatever we want in a way that helps the Creator, creation, and every other human creator do what they want.

The Independent One does not master us as we intend to master Him. Only a taker seizes everything, encroaches everywhere, and kills everyone so that they alone can be the One. Meanwhile, the Maker reveres everything, honors everywhere, and protects everyone so that all might seize the opportunity to make themselves invaluable, irreplaceable, and unreplicable amidst His eternal, world-making partnership.

Our growing independence and mastery are tested when our material body and world are imperiled, damaged, or destroyed to see how we spiritually respond. Of course, that is why the Man was tested in this very manner. No man, other than the Man, has passed or will pass the full test of independent mastery. Not only did the Man have his material body and world destroyed, but his soul was damned to hell for three days. Yet, He remained spiritually unaltered as the Independent Master of Ascension. Then, the Man uplifted his soul and body back to the material realm so all might know Him as the Independent Master from which all would spiritually and materially ascend.

Today, each man has the option of submissively surrendering to the Independent Master of Ascension. Each timeless moment is a man's opportunity for further spiritual ascension into his own likeness of Uniqueness. Then, as a growing independent master, a man may extend his hand to make his inner realm and his personal portion of creation's material realm into their own likeness of his uniqueness. Finally, as the touch of the Independent Master resonates through a man, he may reach out to materially uplift every nearby sovereign so that each might become their own independent, authoritative, and unique world maker.

Chapter 26
Conduits of Interconnecting Love

A man pushes everyone's mind, heart, and body toward depending upon their soul while also pushing everyone's soul toward depending upon God. At the same time, a man also pushes everyone's mind, heart, and body toward independence from any form of external control, including himself, while also pushing every soul toward independence from their own mind, heart, and body. Independence must flow from the spiritual realm, through the inner realm, and out into the material realm, while dependence must flow from the material realm, through the inner realm, and back into the spiritual realm. Our Father's outward-moving love is independent and our mother's inward-moving love is dependent. As the interconnecting conduits between our spiritual Father and material mother, each human being is the intended channel to conduct the Creator's independent love out toward His creation and creation's dependent love back toward her Creator. Therefore, the couple who are using their bodies as the conduits of interconnecting love between our spiritual Father and our material mother will live to weave all back into the eternally affectionate embrace of the first partnership.

Masculine authority flows from God, through humanity, and out to creation. Feminine submission flows from creation, through humanity, and back to God. Therefore, as a man embraces a woman, it is our Father's authoritative love that flows through his body, into his wife's body, and out to creation. Then, as a woman reciprocates, it is our mother's submissive love that flows back through her body, into her husband's body, and to the Creator. Each couple creates their own unique union of interconnecting love. However, the couple who makes their two bodies conduits for the interplay of love between the first partnership will exponentially amplify the passion, pleasure, and power their partnership creates.

The more uniquely a marital union embodies the Creator and creation, the more valuable their union will be to the first partnership in making a race of unique world makers who, together, are perpetually bringing forth a world of unique worlds. Like each individual, each couple must boldly create their own unique position within the original world-making partnership. Then, the Creator and creation will begin to perceive the couple's lifelong, orchestrational effort as indispensable to their eternal, orchestrational effort. The obvious purpose of a marital union is to express two world makers through the orchestration of one shared world. However, the Creator and creation remain deeply invested in every world maker and every world. As a result, each couple who opens their world to the influence of our Father and our mother will be blessed. However, each couple who actively works toward our Father's race of unique world makers and our mother's world of unique worlds will be blessed while also becoming a blessing.

The Creator and creation do not desire a couple's world to become like their world. Our Father and our mother desire a couple's world to become unlike any other world so that they might produce world makers unlike any other. The Creator told the first man and woman to fruitfully multiply because He desires many unique world makers for His eternal world-making partnership. Additionally, creation also resonates with the Creator's zeal, as evidenced by how thoroughly she imbues all human bodies with a passion for biological reproduction. As a couple designs their world toward serving the deepest desires of our spiritual Father and our material mother, they're boldly making their partnership irreplaceable to the first partnership.

Since our inner realm lies in between the Creator's spiritual realm and creation's material realm, the position that the first partnership desires each inner marital union of one flesh to occupy is not a mystery. Boldly seizing the epicenter of orchestration by making oneself and one's marriage essential to the foremost desires of the first partnership is audacious. However, our Creator expects nothing less from any couple who desires inclusion within His eternal, world-making partnership.

The more intentionally a couple crafts their bodies into one united, two-way conduit of reciprocal love for the Creator and creation, the more effectively they'll ennoble and enable all. The more a man radiates God's independent love, the more unstoppable he'll be in making and protecting a race of unique world makers. Similarly, the more a woman resonates with creation's dependent love, the more irresistible she'll be in making and protecting a world of unique worlds.

The male and female bodies want to be conduits for the interplay of love between our Father and our mother. Additionally, both bodies also want to uniquely personify the first partnership. Furthermore, both bodies also want their partnership to meld amidst the embrace of the first partnership so that both independent, interconnected, and interdependent world-making unions will begin growing into one.

As a couple showers everyone with the Creator's independent ennobling love and creation's dependent enabling love, they're pushing and pulling everyone back into the waiting arms of the first partnership. The first man and woman chose to remove themselves—and their descendants—from the loving arms of our Father and our mother. Thanks to the sacrifice of the Man, each couple now has the option of returning themselves—and their descendants—back to the epicenter of interconnecting love.

Our Father pushes each soul toward loving His creation while our mother pulls each body toward loving her Creator. Currently, our Father does not have a material body in the material realm to touch His creation. However, we do. Similarly, our mother does not have a spiritual being to touch her Creator in the spiritual realm. However, we do. Should we desire to orchestrate our own unique world from inside the first couple's world, then offering what we have and who we are to our Father and our mother is the best way to attain the fullness of our world-making intentions.

The first couple wishes to embrace one another around us, with us, and through us so that we might stay with them as they stay with us. Therefore, the couple who make their union into an epicenter of interconnecting love will exert a touch upon everything and everyone that pushes and pulls all toward seeing, feeling, and experiencing what humanity has been missing. As a result, the zeal of a husband and the passion of a wife will awaken to new heights for their union, for the first union, and for every union. Only as a man and a woman live together in serving the deepest desires of the Creator, creation, and every human creator will they uncover their deepest desire in being humanity's epicenter of interconnecting love.

Chapter 27
Eternally Interdependent Partners

In conclusion, a man must seriously consider why he should even bother living as a masculine creator. Although sacrificially serving humanity, creation, and the Creator by protecting the sovereignty, uniqueness, and world-making opportunity of everyone is a noble undertaking, that alone is insufficient to motivate a lifelong masculine effort. Each man must know precisely why he should willingly pay such a price on the behalf of others. Consequently, the only motive big enough to drive a man to endure the lifetime of hardships inherent to becoming a self-defining, co-defining, and global-defining authority is so that he might make the eternally interdependent partners he needs to help him make his unique world.

No man alone may orchestrate the unique body, skill, enterprise, family, team, position, and legacy he needs to fulfill the totality of his world-making intentions. Even takers spend their lives trying to deceive creation and other human creators because they know they cannot make a world that allows them to look, feel, and act like God without partners. Although a masculine creator has no need to deceive creation or other human creators, that does not lessen his need for partners. A masculine creator—who lives in the likeness of the Masculine Creator—knows that the best way to acquire the partners he needs to assist him in making his world is to make world makers.

The bigger and more complex a man's envisioned world, the higher the quality and quantity of world-making partners he'll require. As a result, it is the grandeur of a man's world that determines the grandeur of his drive to be a maker of world makers. Protecting everyone's sovereignty, preserving everyone's uniqueness, and procuring everyone's world-making opportunity—amidst the present age of world takers—will ultimately cost a man his life. Still, the benefit for a masculine creator is to form partnerships with the most profound, potent, and powerful world makers of his day. Moreover, the man who gives his life to protect the sovereignty of every unique one will also recieve the eternally affectionate appreciation of the Unique One.

A man's drive to make world makers for his lifelong, world-making effort comes from the Masculine Creator. The Maker desires to make world makers so He might have the most profound, potent, and powerful partners for His eternal, world-making effort. Although it may seem inconceivable, the Creator desires every soul standing beside Him as an independent, interconnected, and interdependent world-making partner. God seeks a union with everyone who desires to become a unique one and create their own unique world. Through each submissive soul of faith, God is presently making the ideal partners He desires for His eternal, world-making effort. The man who desires to live as a masculine creator amidst the present age will follow the same process to make the ideal partners he desires for his lifelong, world-making effort.

The Creator is up to something big—far bigger than what any of us can presently theorize. The present age is merely God's recruitment phase. However, unlike human recruiters, God is not advertising what He's looking for in a partner. Instead, God wants partners so assured of their value—from receiving His touch as the Valuable One—that they present themselves and the uniqueness they have to offer without request. As finite creators, we may feel wholly incapable of approaching the Infinite One so boldly. However, that is exactly the type of partner God desire. Our Father created the spiritual realm, our inner realm, and creation's material realm to make us into world makers. He expects us to spiritually walk beside Him, inwardly learn from Him, and materially express the unique one we're becoming because of Him. Then, as we mature into our own independent, authoritative, and unique world-making likeness, our Father expects us to present ourselves and the uniqueness we have to offer for inclusion within His eternal, world-making effort.

The Creator is currently keeping tight-lipped about His eternal aspirations. In the same way that a man strategically cultivates unique world makers over the course of decades to attain his grand design, so God is strategically gathering unique world makers to Himself in preparation for His eternal design. God has the plan, and we're currently only in phase one. He expects us to study Him and learn what little He allows us to sense regarding His eternal aspirations. Then, He expects us to make our own plan in a manner that will also support His plan.

God is not interested in us having the right plan. He's only interested in us making our own plan and boldly presenting that to Him in a way that reveals how our plan will also benefit His plan. Eternity will provide us with ample opportunities to improve our plan. Presently, God seeks those who will partner with His plan, with their own plan, while working their plan with dedication, defiance, and determination amidst the present fallen age. We don't have to impress God as an ideal partner today. However, we do have to impress God that we will become an ideal partner in the coming age under His eternal guidance, through our growing authority, and amidst creation's assistance.

The man developing a world-making partnership with God while also working intently on cultivating the greatest world makers of his age will find himself in the enviable position of being surrounded by partners eager to assist him in executing his plan. Since a masculine creator's plan is designed to fulfill the world-making intentions of the Creator, creation, and all human creators, he'll not need to manipulate others into partnering with him. Fallen men exhaust themselves trying to convince others to partner with their plan while trying to hide the fact that their plan is to prohibit everyone else's world-making plan so that they alone might become the One. Conversely, a resurrected man simply offers everyone what they want—his protection for their sovereignty, his preservation of their uniqueness, and his procurement of their world-making opportunity alongside his world within God's world. Like the Masculine Creator, a masculine creator will only unite his world with the worlds of those who have their own plan and boldly present their plan in a way that supports his plan. Every unique one brings forth a unique world producing unique products and services. All worlds rise together amidst a world of unique worlds, especially the world of the man who ensures it all happens. As a result, the man who lives to serve every sovereign will have no shortage of eager, world-making partners.

Since every world maker and their world are unique, a masculine creator cannot dictate to anyone how to be a unique one or how to create their own unique world. Instead, a masculine creator simply protects the sovereignty, uniqueness, and world-making opportunity of everyone. As a result, anyone who benefits amidst a man's protection will rise into an independent, authoritative, and unique world maker. Then, all who benefited will strive, on their own accord, to figure out how they might become a uniquely valuable partner to their masculine creator.

Trying to motivate others to do what they don't want to do is exhausting. A masculine creator acquires the partners he desires for his world-making effort by designing his world to ensure that everyone around him has an opportunity to create their world. Those who take full advantage of a man's protection will rise into the most profound, potent, and powerful world makers of their day while desiring to stay close to the man who's already proven so valuable to their survival, comfort, and orchestration. As a result, the partners a man requires for his lifelong, world-making effort will simply rise into existence all around him.

Only in retrospect will a man realize how impossible it would have been for him to dictate to each one how to become a unique one and create their own unique world that would prove valuable to his world. Only fallen men attempt to make others from the outside in. The Man makes world makers from the inside out. A masculine creator merely ensures that the Man's spiritual work upon each soul is free to rise through each individual's inner realm and out into creation's material realm, free from any form of outside-in meddling.

A masculine creator must know, with absolute certainty, that the only way to find the quality and quantity of partners he requires for his world is to make them. This is the way of the Masculine Creator. Any man who wishes to uniquely embody the Masculine One will spend his life making the independent, authoritative, and unique world-making partners he requires for his life-long, world-making effort. Furthermore, since anyone could end up becoming an irreplaceable partner for his world, a man will find himself protecting the sovereignty, preserving the uniqueness, and procuring the world-making opportunity of everyone.

God is determined not to interfere with any creator's development. Our Maker does not force us to partner with Him. He's even allowed us to have our age of rebellion by simply accepting that anyone dedicated, defiant, and determined enough to partner with Him amidst an ongoing rebellion would certainly be the type of partner He desires for His eternal, world-making effort. From God's perspective, the only thing more dangerous to the development of a unique world maker than living inside a hostile world is being rescued from that hostile world. Even when God did enter our fallen age, He did so to restore our spiritual freedom to choose. Still, He did not interfere with the first man's choice or anyone who desired to persist in making the first man's choice. God is presently looking for submissive souls who will expend the remainder of their doomed days walking at His side in the spiritual realm so they might display the unique one He's making out through their inner realm and into their personal portion of creation's material realm.

The man who lives his life to make world makers provides the Creator, creation, and all humanity with what everyone desires most. The Creator cannot fulfill His recruitment quota without a sovereign who is elevating sovereigns. Creation cannot become her Beloved's world of unique worlds without a creator who is creating creators. And humanity will remain ignorant of the burning drive we all carry without a world maker who is making world makers.

Amidst all the partners a man binds himself to across the course of his life, there is only One who is essential. A man's most zealous partner will always remain the Masculine Creator. In the coming age of creators, the Man will be physically present with the male body He acquired. However, the finite nature of that male body will restrict the Masculine Creator from being materially omnipresent amidst His eternal, world-making partnership. Therefore, God clings most fiercely to any man who displays his commitment to making world makers in the present age because He'll have much need for such men in the age yet to come.

www.ingramcontent.com/pod-product-compliance
Lightning Source LLC
Chambersburg PA
CBHW060743050426
42449CB00008B/1300

9 781941 192047